Rock Block ▶

Etching and aquatint, $27\frac{1}{4} \times 21\frac{1}{4}$ in.

Oxtoby: *Rock Block* is a two-plate coloured
etching and aquatint. Due to the variety of colours,
it takes over three-quarters of an hour to print one
plate. The edition is limited to twenty-five. *Rock
Block* consists of sixteen images based on a few of
the major influences of early rock; the print
assimilates a poster while reflecting the dismissal of
inhibitions, the freedom felt in the early days of rock.

David Sandison

A Dutton **dep** Paperback

Acknowledgements

Design: Ken Vail

Phaidon Press Limited, Littlegate House, St Ebbe's Street, Oxford

Published in the United States of America by E. P. Dutton, New York

First published 1978

ISBN 0 7148 1854 2
Library of Congress Catalog Card No: 78-50831

Printed in Italy by Amilcare Pizzi, SpA, Milan.

I would like to thank Mrs Ann Oxtoby, Dorothy Oxtoby, Norman Stevens, David Hockney, Michael Upton, John Loker, Michael Vaughan, Paul Hockney, Austin Sayer, Ian Wood, Edward Lucie-Smith, William Packer, John Synge, Harry Tatlock Miller, Joe Studholme, Jonathan Morrish, Tom Sheehan, Lady Rushbury, Carl Perkins and Teresa Donellen for their time, advice and assistance—all invaluable to me in the preparation of this book. Also to Mark Ritchie at Phaidon, without whom . . . Thank you all.

Thanks are also due to the following collections and collectors for use of pictures owned by them:

The Tate Gallery, London; The Victoria and Albert Museum and Theatre Museum; The Bradford City Art Gallery; The Leeds City Art Gallery; Whitworth Art Gallery, Manchester; Leonard Bocour; Mr and Mrs B. P. Knox-Peebles; Edward Lucie-Smith; Elton John; John Reid; Bernie Taupin; Jim Collyer; Rod Stewart; Steve Howe; Poons of Covent Garden; Mrs Ann Oxtoby; Dorothy Oxtoby; Jim Capaldi; Steve Winwood; Stan Hardy, Lord and Lady Tamlaw, CBS, Charly Records and Perin Khan.

All etchings are reproduced by kind permission of Editions Alecto. All paintings are reproduced by kind permission of the Redfern Gallery.

Finally, the author and publishers would like to thank Miki Slingsby, who was responsible for the photography, including the cover.

List of Works

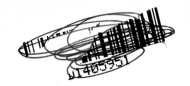

GARY GLITTER: *Glitterin'*. Ballpoint pen.

This book is dedicated to John Henry Oxtoby
and Ann Oxtoby

and to the memories of

Elvis Presley, Gene Vincent, Eddie Cochran,
The Big Bopper, Buddy Holly, Ritchie Valens,
Janis Joplin, Jimi Hendrix, Brian Jones, Jim
Morrison, Gram Parsons, Smiley Lewis,
Frankie Lymon, Otis Redding, King Curtis,
Bobby Parker, Clyde McPhatter, Johnny
Kidd, Marc Bolan, Arthur Crudup, Bobby
Darin, Johnny Burnette, Moon Mullican, and
too many others

Foreword

The illustrations in this book, it goes without saying, are the sole reason for its publication. That the paintings, drawings and etchings of David Oxtoby would one day reach a huge audience in book form was never in doubt— his work is too dramatic and touches too many people's lives to remain on the walls of galleries and museums or in the collections of a few people fortunate enough to be able to buy it.

He is the first modern painter to devote his working life completely to translating the images created by music in a way which is accessible both to the layman and the critic. More specifically, throughout his career he has concentrated on capturing the aural and visual excitement of rock 'n' roll and its performers.

That he has succeeded is obvious from a glance at any of the works reproduced here. That he has thereby performed a great service to this and future generations goes without saying, for while photographs and film may contain some images for eternity, the infrastructures, references and observations which fill Oxtoby's canvases tell those who look closely much more than any number of photographs could.

The biographical introduction, which outlines the events and influences of David Oxtoby's life, is included by way of explanation as to why such an obviously gifted artist should spend his life chronicling the work and influences of other artists.

The advent of rock 'n' roll in the mid-Fifties changed a whole generation's way of life. Few were as deeply affected as Oxtoby himself. He became, and remains, the subtitle of this book: The Eternal Fan.

David Sandison

David Jowett Greaves Oxtoby was born in the village of Horsforth, Yorkshire, at 11.45 a.m. on Sunday, 23 January 1938—'just an Aquarius and just in time for lunch!'

He was a late arrival—his only sister Dorothy being fifteen at the time—but the delight of his parents and the love and attention they were to lavish on him during childhood compensated for the lack of a close sibling. It was a comfortable childhood, the war notwithstanding, in a large Victorian house which still stands back off the Rawdon Road close to the fringes of the Yorkshire moors.

Oxtoby's father, John Henry, was a successful and busy man, chief traveller for a local wholesale carpet company. Oxtoby's mother was, and is, a busy genial woman who doted on a much-wanted son. Daughter of once-wealthy and landed Yorkshire gentry, Ann Oxtoby ensured that the new arrival had everything he needed—and this particular arrival needed a lot, having been born with a chronic bronchial condition. 'We had a really bad time with him', she recalls. 'He cut every tooth with bronchitis and he needed constant nursing'.

Dorothy ended her schooling early to help look after her younger brother and she remembers the panic to get him wrapped up in a mass of blankets whenever the air-raid sirens sounded. Then it would be a dash into the garden bomb shelter with the swaddled baby. Later she would have a constant battle with an energetic and impish boy who, like any child of his age, wanted to get out and about but had to be smothered in warm clothes before he could venture even into the garden.

'I'm afraid in some ways I was more hindrance than help', she admits today. 'I suppose I begrudged him the attention he got and used to chase him around when he should have been taking it easy. But it was mother who carried most of the burden—she'd be up with him all hours when he couldn't sleep or breathe.

Many's the night she had to stay up with him until dawn, with him propped up so he could get air in. It wasn't easy.'

Consecutive winters with pneumonia resulted in the family doctor advising the Oxtobys to take the boy to the west coast where sea air might help his condition, so Ann Oxtoby moved with David to Blackpool for a year. Although he was only eight at the time, she enrolled him in a local school which specialized in art. There were already signs that the young Oxtoby could become a talented artist.

The long hours he'd been forced to spend alone and the fact that toys were hard to come by in wartime Britain meant that Oxtoby, like so many children his age, had to make his own entertainment. At an early age—from the time he discovered that a pencil pushed across a page could make a shape—he'd been an inveterate artist.

The word 'inveterate' is used advisedly because it wasn't just pencils and crayons that he seized to while away the hours. Anything which could make patterns and shapes was grabbed and used. For a long time, until he was broken of the habit, even the family toothpaste had to be locked away out of reach. Left available to the compulsive and enthusiastic artist, it would inevitably finish up all over the bathroom walls and mirrors. He had also discovered plasticine and would enthral his family and friends with tiny, intricate and finely detailed models—galleons, especially, with miniscule portholes, gun-ports, masts, riggings and sails.

Crying Baby. Scraperboard. 1953.

Oxtoby's own memories of that period are dominated by his model-making, drawing, and his father reading to him—the book *Pinocchio* especially. He would listen enthralled to the magical stories, draw his own illustrations, then beg for more. Although he must have known it by heart and grown sick of it, his father always complied and was rewarded in 1970 when Oxtoby did, as a limited edition silkscreen, a beautiful modern frontispiece illustration for *Pinocchio*.

Oxtoby's artistic skill had also been encouraged at the local Featherbank Council Primary School by teacher Bob Gray. Having missed so much formal education because of his illnesses, and thus being behind in most subjects, Bob Gray allowed him to concentrate on art and to entertain the others with paintings and puppet shows.

After that year in Blackpool, Ann Oxtoby and David returned to Horsforth and set about finding a school which would further his artistic talent. And it was eventually decided to send him to Bradford Junior Art School, nine miles away. His art education was to last for the next 14 years. At the school Oxtoby met Norman Stevens. A year older than Oxtoby, Stevens had missed schooling because of numerous operations on his leg, and although Stevens denies it, their first meeting was traumatic for Oxtoby. The way Oxtoby tells it, Norman pulled his pants off and threw him into the girls' play-yard, forcing David to beat a hasty, and undignified retreat. Despite that introduction the two became close friends. They lived near each other and therefore shared bus and car journeys together; they had the same tastes—and the beginnings of what some in the art world have called 'The Bradford Mafia' were founded.

Stevens's memories of Bradford at that time are not as rosy as Oxtoby's, and he still blames staff there for not really doing anything to help his friend who, left to his own devices, preferred to mess around and draw imaginary LP record covers rather than knuckle down to real learning. He just wasn't pushed into realizing his potential. The theory of the Art Schools was a good one; they were places where boys could be taught something which could help them in later life, but Bradford Art School was full of ruffians then.

'Dave and I were in graphics', Stevens recalls, 'and when I moved over to painting they wouldn't let him. A new principal had arrived and he was a real pig to Dave. Actually, he tried to stop me changing courses but I'd already gone to the education authorities and it was too late. Dave was stuck there in graphics, able to walk it with both eyes closed, and he was frustrated. He wanted to move on to other things but he was stuck somewhere else with an idiot head of department who considered himself the college policeman. I'm sure that if Dave had got into

Bill Squires and Friends. Oil painting by Oxtoby, Stevens and Hockney. 1955.

Bradford Rag skiffle group.

painting earlier it would have been easier for him later, especially when he tried to get into the Royal College of Art.'

David Hockney's arrival at Bradford was almost as traumatic for him as the first meeting with Norman Stevens had been for Oxtoby.

They were working in class one day when the door opened and Hockney came in looking like a Russian peasant. He was wearing a big duffle coat, had a huge long scarf, and little wire glasses and a mop of black hair that looked like it had been cut with shears. He tripped over an easel and they all burst out laughing. Oxtoby commented to Stevens: 'Christ, he's a real Boris!' From that day on for a long time David Hockney was known to one and all, including some of the staff, as Boris!

Hockney's own memories of his first encounter with David Oxtoby are less anguished but more pertinent. 'He was one of the first people I noticed when I walked through the door—I'm pretty sure he was wearing a bottle-green Edwardian suit—he was a real Teddy boy in those days. But he was so lively and interesting we became friends straight away.

'When I first met him he was a real yobbo. He never took anything seriously, but by the time we left Bradford his attitude had changed.'

John Loker is more specific. He'd entered the school a year later, but had been moved up to Oxtoby's graphics class because there were only two in his year—him and Peter Kay.

'I actually went and complained when we were put in with him', he says. 'It was full of

absolute lunatics—and he was unbelievable! He used to drive us round the twist—he'd sit at the back banging his knees and making bass noises while you'd be trying to work. And he'd do crazy things like paint bits of plaster the same colour as the ceiling, wait until you were busy and lob them in the air so they landed on you from above. You'd think the ceiling was coming down—it was impossible! He once emptied someone's briefcase and nailed it to a desk . . . and this used to go on all day. It used to drive us mad!'

It probably drove the school staff mad too, and Oxtoby was left pretty well to get on with whatever he chose. The first pieces of work dealing with music started to appear. At that time, student skiffle and jazz groups apart, his preoccupation was with the raucous excitement of the emerging rockers—Presley, Haley, Jerry Lee Lewis and Fats Domino especially. Sketches and drawings flowed from him like a torrent and he made for the places where the music was most played—dance-halls, fairgrounds and cafes with juke boxes.

Although they spent a lot of time together and the others often stayed over at the ever-welcom-

ing Oxtoby house, a subtle distance had grown between Oxtoby and his contemporaries. They weren't the kind to hang around dance-halls and pinball machines.

The hard work Stevens and David Hockney were putting in was due mainly to lecturer Derek Stafford, then only 24 years old and fresh from the Royal College of Art in London. He pushed them, determined to prove that not all the Bradford crowd were hopeless cases. Oxtoby would sneak out from graphics as often as he could to join his friends in life-drawing (something he did enjoy and apply himself to), but they were improving far faster than he.

To his credit, Oxtoby was aware of the discrepancy and made efforts to catch up in whatever way he could. He'd carry a sketchbook with him no matter where he went and be the despair of friends who'd carry on a lengthy conversation with him on a bus only to discover that he'd heard nothing, so intent was he on drawing the head of a person in front of them!

Despite his hard work, while all his friends were accepted by the Royal College of Art, Oxtoby was turned down.

Oxtoby's plan had been simple: apply to the Royal College as a graphics student, get in and then move over to join Norman Stevens and David Hockney in painting. It had never occurred to him that the Royal College of Art would turn him down. But they had and he had to do a rapid re-think.

He had by now finished at Bradford, of course, graduating with a certificate to say he'd completed their course to the faculty's satisfaction(!); so that gave him a year to work hard at his drawing, get some kind of job to tide him over financially, and re-apply the following year. He got a job labouring for the local council, and did scenery painting for the Grand Theatre in Leeds. He also worked on some of the decorations for the famous Blackpool illuminations, that particularly British explosion of light and colour which graces the North's most popular resort during the summer months. Oxtoby's main task was to do a 175-feet-long reproduction of Botticelli's *Birth of Venus*, but he also decorated a huge ex-Air Force nissen hut for a local chicken-farm entrepeneur who used it for lavish beer feasts. And all the time he worked at improving his drawing and building up a portfolio which would get him into the Royal College.

It didn't.

'I passed the practical examination with very high marks and got an interview', he says. 'I still don't know what it was that let me down. Maybe they were looking for teaching material. . . . Disheartened but not beaten, he returned home. The next few months saw him again working at the Grand Theatre in Leeds as a scenery painter and lighting electrician. And then he met up with Michael Vaughan one day in Bradford, and was urged by him to apply and I knew a few people were a bit suspicious about this long-haired yob who'd suddenly appeared. It must have put them in a funny position because I know I felt it, the responsibility I mean.'

'But the erotic drawings that I did were a reaction to the kind of society that allowed Little Rock and Selma to happen. They were a reaction by me against what was going on in Alabama. People were getting shot and lynched, bombs were being thrown into churches and killing babies. I just had to make some sort of statement.'

Minneapolis also introduced him to Leonard Bocour, inventor of Aquatec, the polymer emulsion paint. He visited Minneapolis to deliver a lecture, struck up a friendship with Oxtoby, bought a few pictures and then kept in touch. A few years later he offered Oxtoby some paint as a trade for another picture and since then Oxtoby has had a regular supply of Aquatec in return for occasional works. He now works almost exclusively with Aquatec for his painted work, preferring its drying speed and staying power to those of the doubtful and slow oil-based materials. Aquatec's brilliant and more basic colours are also ideally-suited to the strident Fifties feel he aims for in those pictures.

At the Easter break of 1965 Oxtoby returned to Britain, fully intending to return to Minneapolis. But his return was made impossible by a notification of possible conscription into the American armed forces.

'The letter I got said that if I was on vacation,

Selma. One of a series. Ballpoint pen. 1964.

they wanted me back for the Vietnam war. If I was working, on the other hand, and wanted to renounce my claim to American citizenship—I was on an immigration visa—they wanted to know. As the idea of maybe dying in Vietnam didn't really thrill me, I wrote back to them saying I was working in Britain again.'

Although he had enjoyed it, the Minneapolis sojourn had thrown Oxtoby off-balance somewhat. While he'd been away, contemporaries like Hockney had captured the headlines he'd once dominated. He didn't need a job, but he did need time to re-think and get down to work.

To keep him occupied, Michael Vaughan suggested that Oxtoby take a Fellowship at Manchester College of Art. He, John Loker and Norman Stevens were already working in Manchester. It would be like old times.

Oxtoby liked the idea. 'I thought it would be nice, so after a holiday in Spain I went to Manchester. But there was nothing for me to do there and I got bored after a few weeks and my work wasn't going well. I couldn't just hang around to see what happened, so I came back to London.'

In London he was re-united with Michael Upton, who was teaching painting at Maidstone College of Art while David Hockney was teaching etching. He knew that Gerald De-Rose, Head of Fine Art, had been keen to snare Oxtoby for some time, so he suggested that the two meet. They did, shook hands on a relationship agreeable to them both and Oxtoby started a job which was to be his until 1972 when his final climactic illness forced him to quit teaching.

The first symptom of that illness which was to get worse and worse, mystify a veritable horde of specialists and make painting an impossibility for more than four years, was an aggravating and discomfiting skin rash on his hands. Nothing to get worried about, he was told. Probably dermatitis. Take this cream—it'll go away.

It didn't, of course, but got progressively nastier. His hands became a mass of open bleeding sores and Oxtoby was forced to wear bandages and gloves not only to mask his condition from the world, but also to avoid the pigment in paint his doctors thought was to blame. It must have been like painting with boxing gloves on.

But while he was able to teach at Maidstone, travelling down from his flat in Notting Hill Gate a couple of times a week, David enjoyed himself. In a strange way it was, he says, like being back at Bradford. 'Gerry De-Rose had quite a little dictatorship going and I needed a no-nonsense and structured work environment like that. Gerry was very involved in drawing—he was known for it, and I've always thought that drawing is the best foundation for so many other things.

'If you can make a drawing work structurally, you can make a piece of sculpture from it. If you

can make a figure stand on the paper and work, you can do practically anything with it. It's not the drawing itself but what can come from it.

'Take the crowd who were with me at Bradford, for instance. We all work in completely different fields now, but the thing we have in common is that we can all draw. We all have that foundation—and that's what I have always believed in as a first principle.

'Apart from that, I don't think I pushed any particular philosophy at the kids when I was teaching at Maidstone. I never thought I had the right. I taught technicalities and whatever the kids did with them was up to them, not me. But I believed that if I taught them how to draw, at least they'd have that starting point.'

While his health lasted, Oxtoby also threw himself back into London rock club life. Newest and biggest magnet for him at this time was the Bag o' Nails, just off the famous Carnaby Street. Very much a watering-hole for off-duty rock stars, it was full of images, noise and the fun Oxtoby was seeking.

'I'd go three, maybe four times a week', he says. 'I had the idea that one had to participate physically in the musical experience. You had to dance to it, really get involved. On top of that I was stoned out of my head most of the time, so I was prepared to get involved more readily. That's the first time I really met a lot of people in the rock business. Until then I'd avoided meeting people because I thought they created their images aurally and meeting them would get in the way of what I was trying to do—their physical reality would overpower the aural aspects. But I found it didn't happen that way, and in fact it made me more sympathetic to their on-stage and on-record images.

'Jimi Hendrix, for instance, who I knew reasonably well at that time, was an incredibly shy and quiet little guy when I knew him. He

Bill Squires and Friends. Oil painting by Oxtoby, Stevens and Hockney. 1955.

Bradford Rag skiffle group.

painting earlier it would have been easier for him later, especially when he tried to get into the Royal College of Art.'

David Hockney's arrival at Bradford was almost as traumatic for him as the first meeting with Norman Stevens had been for Oxtoby.

They were working in class one day when the door opened and Hockney came in looking like a Russian peasant. He was wearing a big duffle coat, had a huge long scarf, and little wire glasses and a mop of black hair that looked like it had been cut with shears. He tripped over an easel and they all burst out laughing. Oxtoby commented to Stevens: 'Christ, he's a real Boris!' From that day on for a long time David Hockney was known to one and all, including some of the staff, as Boris!

Hockney's own memories of his first encounter with David Oxtoby are less anguished but more pertinent. 'He was one of the first people I noticed when I walked through the door—I'm pretty sure he was wearing a bottle-green Edwardian suit—he was a real Teddy boy in those days. But he was so lively and interesting we became friends straight away.

'When I first met him he was a real yobbo. He never took anything seriously, but by the time we left Bradford his attitude had changed.'

John Loker is more specific. He'd entered the school a year later, but had been moved up to Oxtoby's graphics class because there were only two in his year—him and Peter Kay.

'I actually went and complained when we were put in with him', he says. 'It was full of

absolute lunatics—and he was unbelievable! He used to drive us round the twist—he'd sit at the back banging his knees and making bass noises while you'd be trying to work. And he'd do crazy things like paint bits of plaster the same colour as the ceiling, wait until you were busy and lob them in the air so they landed on you from above. You'd think the ceiling was coming down—it was impossible! He once emptied someone's briefcase and nailed it to a desk . . . and this used to go on all day. It used to drive us mad!'

It probably drove the school staff mad too, and Oxtoby was left pretty well to get on with whatever he chose. The first pieces of work dealing with music started to appear. At that time, student skiffle and jazz groups apart, his preoccupation was with the raucous excitement of the emerging rockers—Presley, Haley, Jerry Lee Lewis and Fats Domino especially. Sketches and drawings flowed from him like a torrent and he made for the places where the music was most played—dance-halls, fairgrounds and cafes with juke boxes.

Although they spent a lot of time together and the others often stayed over at the ever-welcom-

ing Oxtoby house, a subtle distance had grown between Oxtoby and his contemporaries. They weren't the kind to hang around dance-halls and pinball machines.

The hard work Stevens and David Hockney were putting in was due mainly to lecturer Derek Stafford, then only 24 years old and fresh from the Royal College of Art in London. He pushed them, determined to prove that not all the Bradford crowd were hopeless cases. Oxtoby would sneak out from graphics as often as he could to join his friends in life-drawing (something he did enjoy and apply himself to), but they were improving far faster than he.

To his credit, Oxtoby was aware of the discrepancy and made efforts to catch up in whatever way he could. He'd carry a sketchbook with him no matter where he went and be the despair of friends who'd carry on a lengthy conversation with him on a bus only to discover that he'd heard nothing, so intent was he on drawing the head of a person in front of them!

Despite his hard work, while all his friends were accepted by the Royal College of Art, Oxtoby was turned down.

Oxtoby's plan had been simple: apply to the Royal College as a graphics student, get in and then move over to join Norman Stevens and David Hockney in painting. It had never occurred to him that the Royal College of Art would turn him down. But they had and he had to do a rapid re-think.

He had by now finished at Bradford, of course, graduating with a certificate to say he'd completed their course to the faculty's satisfaction(!); so that gave him a year to work hard at his drawing, get some kind of job to tide him over financially, and re-apply the following year. He got a job labouring for the local council, and did scenery painting for the Grand Theatre in Leeds. He also worked on some of the decorations for the famous Blackpool illuminations, that particularly British explosion of light and colour which graces the North's most popular resort during the summer months. Oxtoby's main task was to do a 175-feet-long reproduction of Botticelli's *Birth of Venus*, but he also decorated a huge ex-Air Force nissen hut for a local chicken-farm entrepeneur who used it for lavish beer feasts. And all the time he worked at improving his drawing and building up a portfolio which would get him into the Royal College.

It didn't.

'I passed the practical examination with very high marks and got an interview', he says. I still don't know what it was that let me down. Maybe they were looking for teaching material. . . . Disheartened but not beaten, he returned home. The next few months saw him again working at the Grand Theatre in Leeds as a scenery painter and lighting electrician. And then he met up with Michael Vaughan one day in Bradford, and was urged by him to apply

Fifties Sketchbook 1. Mixed medium, 37 × 26¾ in.

for the Royal Academy of Art. Vaughan was a year or so younger than David, and although they were on little more than nodding terms he had admired Oxtoby and his work for some time. He was sure the Academy would take him. It was certainly worth a try, anyway. At that time, in the late Fifties, the Royal Academy was very much the bastion of the British art establishment and not rated as a modern-minded teaching school. But it was London, it was a chance and the two applied.

Oxtoby spent that summer in Hastings, in a cottage which had been rented in the southern sea resort by John Loker, David Hockney and Peter Kay — all three conscientious objectors working out the time they should have spent doing National Service, doing public service work instead. Loker and Kay were working on a farm, Hockney was a hospital porter. Oxtoby joined them. Stevens came down from London some weekends and by the summer the Oxtoby portfolio was good enough for the Royal Academy to give him a place. Michael Vaughan had been accepted too, and thus became a member of the ex-Bradford clique.

Oxtoby in fact started at the Royal Academy just as Loker, Hockney and Kay started at the Royal College of Art. Stevens, on the other hand, was just finishing his course and went back north to a teaching post in Manchester. The others decided to set up house together in London and found a flat in Earls Court, that west London mass of sleazy hotels, bed-and-breakfast joints and London's first true bedsitter ghetto.

Although they all laugh about it now, that flat sounds appalling, even taking into account the fact that they were eking out a living on grants and had to make do with whatever they could afford — which was little. 'It was just one room', Oxtoby relates, 'in which there was Pete Kay, John Loker and myself. I slept in a part of the room that was partitioned off, although it was so thin you could lie in bed talking to the others without raising your voice. Dave Hockney slept outside in a kind of shed — I think it was cheaper for him that way!'

'With three pretty scruffy herberts in a room only fifteen feet square, it was obviously a right mess most of the time. It used to be my job to wake Dave Hockney up — he was terrible at getting up in the mornings! I'd go down into the garden and bang on his door, and he used to do that trick of knocking on the floor with his shoe to make you think he was on the move.'

When Hockney was at last up and about, the four of them would walk the mile or so together to South Kensington and the Royal College of Art; and Oxtoby would then walk on to the Academy in Piccadilly — another two miles or so. It wasn't just a matter of saving pennies (although that was obviously important), but the Academy started later and he had a little time in hand.

His first few weeks were a disappointment and promised a dull four years. 'We had to do life drawing for the first three months and it all seemed a bit dead, a bit flat', he remembers. 'Everything the name of the Academy conjured up at that time, the Establishment, dusty old buildings full of dusty old people, seemed to be true in those first few days.'

'Then, one day this old guy came into the class with a walking stick—the absolute image of what the Academy was supposed to be. He walked up behind this professional virgin of a girl and said: "I don't know what you're trying to do, love, but it's like pissing against Niagara!"

'I thought "That's it! Someone here's for real". The guy was Fleetwood Walker, a friend of Sir Henry Rushbury who was Keeper of the Academy. I got on with them like a house on fire—they were both from Birmingham and they were so young—young men in old bodies. They accepted what I was doing immediately. I adored them and they were good to me. In fact, if it wasn't for the help and encouragement I got from Sir Henry and Fleetwood Walker at the Academy, I don't think I'd be where I am today.'

The next four years were highly enjoyable. With constructive and constant advice from Sir Henry and Fleetwood Walker, Oxtoby thrived on a diet of work and play. Michael Vaughan became a good close friend and after a term at Earls Court, Oxtoby moved out to Tooting to share the first of a number of flats with him. And it was through this friendship that Oxtoby was to discover motorbiking. They spent the next three summers biking around Europe and working together.

'Mick was forever getting old bikes and taking them apart to fix or to use parts for other bikes. There were bits in the kitchen, in the lounge, in the toilet. I'd wake up looking through parts of an engine.

'Inevitably Mick suggested I get something as a runabout. He knew just the bike in Bradford, so next time we went up he took me to this garage and there was this 650 cc Triumph Thunderbird—it was huge! We went out on the moors with it and I rode it up and down a bit, then Mick drove it back into Bradford in the middle of the rush hour. We got to some lights and he jumped off. "Right!", he said, "You're on your own—I'm off to the pictures!"

'There I was, sitting on this damn big machine I'd only ridden on quiet country roads for a few minutes, and I had to get home. I soon got the hang of it though and two days later I was done for speeding!'

Oxtoby's image at the time was hardly Royal Academy. Big, burly, bearded and motorcycle-bound, he'd roar about London looking for action. And it was with Michael Upton, a contemporary at the Academy, that he found most of it. With Birmingham-born Upton, Oxtoby threw himself into the exploding world

of London music. They spent two or three nights most weeks in rock clubs—most especially The Flamingo, in Soho's Wardour Street. 'I think we found a corresponding energy to ours in the music at that time', explains Upton. 'You must remember that a lot of the old traditional values in art were going to the wall. We were right in the middle of abstract expressionism and there were all kinds of things going on—burning canvases, stamping on them . . . and William Green was riding bikes over his canvases at the Royal College.

'I think all that related to what David and I saw happening in music. It's very much synonymous with the breakthrough of people like *The Stones*, *Eric Burdon and The Animals* and people like that. Most people had been into jazz until then—but these people were breaking rules as well.

'We lived at a terrible pace, and I think David's ill-health later was partly as a result of all that. We'd often do a straight 24 hours at a time, going from clubs back to the Academy, then on to clubs again the next evening. David's energy levels were much higher than mine anyway, and he used to work like a demon!'

To say that Oxtoby threw himself into his work is in no way an overstatement. At the flat he shared with Michael Vaughan, the rooms

Vaughan and Oxtoby and Thunderbird outside the Royal Academy Schools. 1962.

were packed with pictures. At the Academy he was completing three or four pictures a day—great experimental slashes of colour and shape—and more often than not his other nights would be spent in the noisy dark of clubs hearing the new sounds being made by exciting young musicians.

'I think a lot of his energy then and now has a lot to do with his background', explains Upton. 'I don't know sometimes whether it's necessarily a good thing, but he does have that work ethic peculiar to the north of England. I remember him referring to painting one time as "graft"—as in "a hard day's graft"—and I know Norman uses the word too. It also implies a kind of suspicion of southern culture-based effeteness.

'All I know about that time was that he used to fill the place with paint. When he was at work, it was best to place yourself well away from him

you are invited to the first exhibition of paintings by David Oxtoby on Wednesday 22 May 1963 from 5 to 7 pm at Gallery One 16 North Audley Street Grosvenor Square London WI HYDe Park 5880

Oxtoby, Upton, Procktor and Vaughan at Upton's show at the Piccadilly Gallery. 1967.

or you'd get the residue of his enthusiasm on your own work! He covered everything in paint, and when he'd run out of the more usual surfaces like canvas and hardboard, he'd tear up telephone books and use the pages.

'You also have to consider that David is, and always has been, something of a romantic. His manner and style of painting have always been very romantically orientated. The clubs fulfilled two basic needs—they provided the kind of music we could get off on, but they also provided an excuse to live a reverse and very nineteenth-century romantic-novel life. It was all part of that mystique of reversing the normal living pattern and kicking against the traditional and accepted—only David got into it far more than most of us.'

But there had been a change in Oxtoby's attitudes. Work had become the single most important driving force in his life and in 1963 he crammed the annual Academy students' exhibition with so many works it resembled not so much a survey of the student body's efforts during that year but an Oxtoby one-man show with a few other people's work thrown in. And it wasn't just quantity, for he won six special prizes for the pictures.

Victor Musgrave, owner of the important

Oxtoby with Buttercup Powell (widow of Bud Powell) at his second New York exhibition, 1967.

Gallery One (later to be taken over by Robert Fraser), saw that exhibition, was impressed, and offered David a real one-man show at his place. Among the critics who came to see and marvel at the bold stark canvases Oxtoby gave Musgrave for that exhibition was Edward Lucie-Smith. He recalls their impact at the time:

'What interested me most about them was that while everyone was going on about the popular media, they were mostly doing so from the outside and making academic portraits of what they thought the popular media were about. David seemed to be someone who was trying to plug in directly to what was really happening.

'The pop mafia at the time remained, for all their pretensions of working-class backgrounds, very middle-class in their attitudes. But David Oxtoby was, if you like, sitting square-eyed in front of the TV because it really was what he liked to do. He was involved in the pop thing in a much less self-conscious way than anyone else.

'Those early Gallery One pictures were very stark, with the kind of finish Patrick Hughes gets now. We weren't used to that kind of art then—the idea of that much rawness hadn't come in yet.'

The London art world, aware that a revolution was happening all around them, were desperately keen to find and make new stars. They made one such star out of Oxtoby. The Nordness Gallery in New York took his pictures early in 1964 and flew him to the States to promote their show. Oxtoby used the opportunity to spend as much time as he could in Harlem, hearing first-hand the music on which he had based most of his work since his teens.

After New York, it was Stockholm and further acclaim, then back to Lewes on England's south coast and a sell-out triumph, followed by another London show—this time at The Redfern Gallery. It was heady stuff, six one-man shows before he'd even finished studying at the Academy!

But even headier things were in store. While he'd been in America for the Nordness show he'd been approached by Arnold Herstand, principal of the Minneapolis College of Art. How, he asked, would the 26-year-old Oxtoby like to become Visiting Professor of Painting at his college?

Oxtoby took a trip out to Minneapolis to see the place for himself and learned that he had been recommended for the post by none other than Sir Basil Spence, doyen of British architecture, who had recently designed a new wing for the college. He was a close friend of Sir Henry Rushbury and already owned a number of Oxtobys. Asked to recommend a young painter he'd had no hesitation in mentioning David's name.

Oxtoby caused quite a furore in Minneapolis in the nine months he was actively teaching there. It was the height of the British pop

invasion of America so anything from England—especially from *The Beatles*' own north—was super-special. He also had long hair while most of his students were still fraternity-and-sorority-conscious crewcut boys and cheerleading girls.

Local television and radio stations seized on this way-out guest celebrity, as far removed from the accepted image of a 'Prof'—albeit a painting prof—as anything they could have dreamed up themselves in the silly season. He was soon the object of a media build-up and did what every young man in that position would do—made the most of it. The people wanted him to be outrageous so he obliged.

However, Minneapolis College of Art suffered by it. Their Visiting Professor completed only two canvases while he was there. He was too busy living up to the image he and the local newshounds had built, and working on a series of explicit erotic drawings (which sold extremely well) and a collection of angry satirical cartoons based on the civil rights march atrocities centred around Selma, Alabama. In them, plump, smug, southern belles disembowelled and decapitated picaninnies while bald-headed eagles picked at impaled black adult carcasses. They were beautiful and angry, with more than a hint of what Ralph Steadman would one day do with his political cartoons, and they were the only pictures Oxtoby has ever done in his life which were not inspired by music. Rauschenburg felt they were the most disturbing drawings he had ever seen. All that survives as proof of their brilliance and the battering they must have given Minneapolis in 1964/5 are a few photographs—the originals were all snapped up by Minnesotans.

For the Christmas of 1964 Oxtoby sent one of his milder erotic drawings to Sir Henry Rushbury and received a charming letter in reply from the now-retired Keeper. Sir Henry was

obviously amused by the drawing and news of his protégé's progress, but took time to lecture David on a few artistic points the drawing had raised in his mind: 'I always think artists, if they are frank and fearless, have a unique opportunity of releasing all their hopes and fears, their passions and their laughter, in their work', he wrote. 'You apparently have had a real go—and I hope the Americans are admiring and buying your amusement. . . . I liked the one you sent me. The design and the life in the line brought back to me the memory of William Blake and Aubrey Beardsley—no mean artists—as well as old Uncle Bosch. It must be a great change to reduce your statement in size and to alter your medium so utterly: this is a good exercise and develops the Oxtoby scope of expression. After all, Durer and Rembrandt did some amazing things no bigger than postcard size.'

The letter, dated 9 February 1965 and postmarked Lewes, Sussex (to where Sir Henry and Lady Rushbury had retired), ended on a sad note to the exile.

'After three years of painful half-life, Fleetwood Walker died last week', he wrote. 'We were boys together and it's a sad moment when the break comes.' To Oxtoby, miles away in the depths of a Minneapolis winter, it was a sad moment too. He had fond memories of an irascible, kindly, warm and educated man who took time and trouble with students he liked.

Another letter from that same period contained further advice which Oxtoby accepted, took to heart and still holds as a basic philosophy for work and life: 'At my age I have lost my way in the maze of expressions of the new idiom which seem to change every Thursday! It must be fun to be in it and to do it, but it seems a load of codswallop to me. I suppose that's how it should be. You are one of the few whose work I respect, for I know that behind it all is wit and fun and an excellent sense of design—and a lovely colour sense which never deserts you.

'You are a gay lad, so don't let the intellectuals get at you and turn you into a parrot, talking and thinking their jargon. Before you know where you are the computors will take over. You'll be feeding the machine with colours and canvas and some bald-headed scientist will press buttons. Out will spew abstracts galore, hundreds of them—and then where are you? The fun is good while it lasts, but life is a long affair.'

So have constructive fun he did. Although Minneapolis was (and is) hardly the centre of the north American art world, Oxtoby was able to take a few open-minded students under his wing and nurture their talents. It was a responsibility he was aware of and did his best to meet.

'I felt as if I had to do something right for the kids and the college', he recalls. 'You see, I was very aware that I was not much older than most of the students—only a couple of years or so—

and I knew a few people were a bit suspicious about this long-haired yob who'd suddenly appeared. It must have put them in a funny position because I know I felt it, the responsibility I mean.'

'But the erotic drawings that I did were a reaction to the kind of society that allowed Little Rock and Selma to happen. They were a reaction by me against what was going on in Alabama. People were getting shot and lynched, bombs were being thrown into churches and killing babies. I just had to make some sort of statement.'

Minneapolis also introduced him to Leonard Bocour, inventor of Aquatec, the polymer emulsion paint. He visited Minneapolis to deliver a lecture, struck up a friendship with Oxtoby, bought a few pictures and then kept in touch. A few years later he offered Oxtoby some paint as a trade for another picture and since then Oxtoby has had a regular supply of Aquatec in return for occasional works. He now works almost exclusively with Aquatec for his painted work, preferring its drying speed and staying power to those of the doubtful and slow oil-based materials. Aquatec's brilliant and more basic colours are also ideally-suited to the strident Fifties feel he aims for in those pictures.

At the Easter break of 1965 Oxtoby returned to Britain, fully intending to return to Minneapolis. But his return was made impossible by a notification of possible conscription into the American armed forces.

'The letter I got said that if I was on vacation,

Selma. One of a series. Ballpoint pen. 1964.

they wanted me back for the Vietnam war. If I was working, on the other hand, and wanted to renounce my claim to American citizenship — I was on an immigration visa — they wanted to know. As the idea of maybe dying in Vietnam didn't really thrill me, I wrote back to them saying I was working in Britain again.'

Although he had enjoyed it, the Minneapolis sojourn had thrown Oxtoby off-balance somewhat. While he'd been away, contemporaries like Hockney had captured the headlines he'd once dominated. He didn't need a job, but he did need time to re-think and get down to work.

To keep him occupied, Michael Vaughan suggested that Oxtoby take a Fellowship at Manchester College of Art. He, John Loker and Norman Stevens were already working in Manchester. It would be like old times.

Oxtoby liked the idea. 'I thought it would be nice, so after a holiday in Spain I went to Manchester. But there was nothing for me to do there and I got bored after a few weeks and my work wasn't going well. I couldn't just hang around to see what happened, so I came back to London.'

In London he was re-united with Michael Upton, who was teaching painting at Maidstone College of Art while David Hockney was teaching etching. He knew that Gerald De-Rose, Head of Fine Art, had been keen to snare Oxtoby for some time, so he suggested that the two meet. They did, shook hands on a relationship agreeable to them both and Oxtoby started a job which was to be his until 1972 when his final climactic illness forced him to quit teaching.

The first symptom of that illness which was to get worse and worse, mystify a veritable horde of specialists and make painting an impossibility for more than four years, was an aggravating and discomfiting skin rash on his hands. Nothing to get worried about, he was told. Probably dermatitis. Take this cream — it'll go away.

It didn't, of course, but got progressively nastier. His hands became a mass of open bleeding sores and Oxtoby was forced to wear bandages and gloves not only to mask his condition from the world, but also to avoid the pigment in paint his doctors thought was to blame. It must have been like painting with boxing gloves on.

But while he was able to teach at Maidstone, travelling down from his flat in Notting Hill Gate a couple of times a week, David enjoyed himself. In a strange way it was, he says, like being back at Bradford. 'Gerry De-Rose had quite a little dictatorship going and I needed a no-nonsense and structured work environment like that. Gerry was very involved in drawing — he was known for it, and I've always thought that drawing is the best foundation for so many other things.

'If you can make a drawing work structurally, you can make a piece of sculpture from it. If you

can make a figure stand on the paper and work, you can do practically anything with it. It's not the drawing itself but what can come from it.

'Take the crowd who were with me at Bradford, for instance. We all work in completely different fields now, but the thing we have in common is that we can all draw. We all have that foundation — and that's what I have always believed in as a first principle.

'Apart from that, I don't think I pushed any particular philosophy at the kids when I was teaching at Maidstone. I never thought I had the right. I taught technicalities and whatever the kids did with them was up to them, not me. But I believed that if I taught them how to draw, at least they'd have that starting point.'

While his health lasted, Oxtoby also threw himself back into London rock club life. Newest and biggest magnet for him at this time was the Bag o' Nails, just off the famous Carnaby Street. Very much a watering-hole for off-duty rock stars, it was full of images, noise and the fun Oxtoby was seeking.

'I'd go three, maybe four times a week', he says. 'I had the idea that one had to participate physically in the musical experience. You had to dance to it, really get involved. On top of that I was stoned out of my head most of the time, so I was prepared to get involved more readily. That's the first time I really met a lot of people in the rock business. Until then I'd avoided meeting people because I thought they created their images aurally and meeting them would get in the way of what I was trying to do — their physical reality would overpower the aural aspects. But I found it didn't happen that way, and in fact it made me more sympathetic to their on-stage and on-record images.

'Jimi Hendrix, for instance, who I knew reasonably well at that time, was an incredibly shy and quiet little guy when I knew him. He wasn't the great phallic god he projected to the public. It was the same with Steve Winwood and the others in *Traffic*. They came on as a very powerful band, but off-stage Steve's a very cool customer.'

The music of *Traffic* and more specifically Steve Winwood, the group's founder, leading light, voice and focal point, provided the basis of a major Oxtoby show in 1972 at the Institute of Contemporary Arts.

Entitled '*Oxtoby Into Traffic*', it consisted of 150 pencil, coloured pencil, felt-tip and ball-point pen drawings, all variations on a central theme David first spotted in a photograph of *Traffic* saxophonist Chris Wood which high-lighted the keys of Wood's sax-bell. David isolated that section of the photo, blew it up and found a ready-made image to use as a starting point.

It was a very brave show, not only artistically but also personally. The previous two years had seen two major crises developing in Oxtoby's life which would have made most men sink into a miasma of self-pity and self-imposed inacti-vity. His father, to whom he had grown very close, was dying. Suffering from a debilitating and humiliating prostate condition, John Henry Oxtoby had been forced into retirement at the age of 79. Cancer had not yet been confirmed, but was suspected by all.

For his part, Oxtoby was suffering an advanc-ing and bewildering weakness. It was no longer a question of his condition being confined to a skin rash. He was now losing a frightening amount of weight—more than 56 lbs in less than a year—and lacked the energy sometimes to walk the short uphill distance from Maidstone rail station to the college in one go. Tests continued, and continued to be inconclusive, but by an extraordinary chance it was John Loker who suggested diabetes, a diagnosis subsequently confirmed.

Oxtoby told his sister of his condition the day she called him to tell him that their father had finally been given a time limit, and she—not wishing to burden their mother with a double weight—kept the secret for close to a year.

Oxtoby: In their chosen field, *Traffic* were without doubt the best and most under-rated English band. These ballpoint pen drawings were executed during the five years I spent on visual interpretations of *Traffic's* complex interwoven rhythms and musical tones—a combination of English countryside mytho-logy, rock and jazz conceived in a very classical manner. Hear *Where The Eagle Flies*. My pictures were purely a gut response to their 'pythagorean shapes and equal temperaments'. I love the timeless quality Steve Winwood manages to create and sympathize with his attitude to success—I learned in the early Sixties that success brings with it many pitfalls. I feel a great affinity with Jim Capaldi's point of view: do your thing and enjoy it. What's Chris Wood doing now?

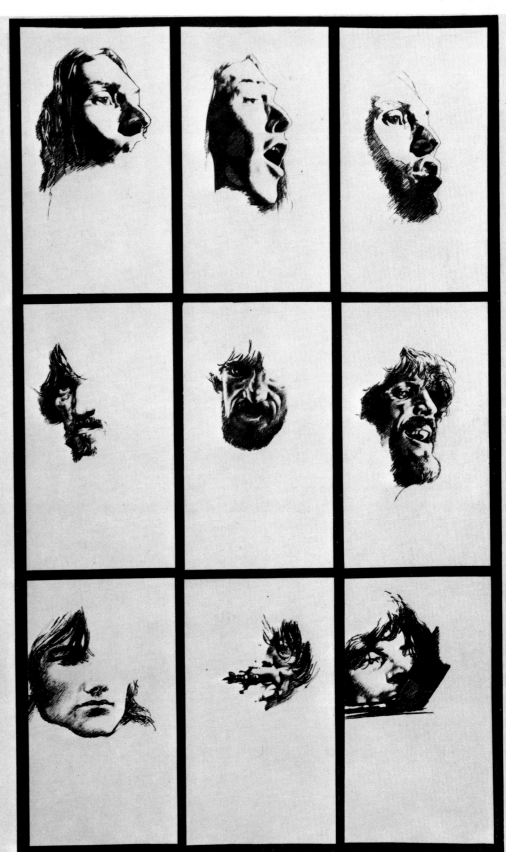

David's father died just before Christmas 1972 unaware that his son was also badly ill. Despite all the pain and weakness he was suffering during that time, David went to Horsforth and painted the only portrait of his life. It is a beautiful picture of John Henry sitting in his favourite armchair and now hangs in the dining room of the family home.

His father's death was the final straw for Oxtoby and he collapsed. Back in London, he was rushed to nearby St Mary's Hospital and there spent a bewildered Christmas. All his friends, however, rallied round and continually visited him. Hockney flooded the hospital with flowers. It was at this time that Oxtoby, as a result of an unhappy love affair, destroyed all the existing pictures from the *Traffic* show. The only examples of that period which do therefore exist are the few that were sold or given away to friends and a handful sent to the Baukunst Gallery in Cologne for a show early in 1973.

By the end of the year Oxtoby's condition had deteriorated and he was taken back into St Mary's for his medication to be stabilized. David Hockney was back in London and visited regularly—and Norman Stevens pressured the bed-ridden Oxtoby into an exercise which was to open up a whole new range of possibilities for him. One day he brought him a copper plate and said he wanted an etching out of David by his next visit.

That first etching—of *Traffic*'s Jim Capaldi—was a rough effort and Stevens's pull of it was hurried and crude. But when Oxtoby saw the finished product he was enthralled and asked for more plates, just as Stevens had predicted.

The idea had come to him as a result of discussions with two young printers, John Crossley and Jim Collyer. They had recently left fine art printers Editions Alecto to start their own JC Editions and were looking for artists to publish. In the late Sixties Jim Collyer had seen and been smitten by the pictures in an Oxtoby show held at the Redfern, so the idea of Oxtoby doing some etchings for them was especially appealing to him.

Norman Stevens had reservations. He knew that Oxtoby would take to etching like a duck to water, but was also aware of the inherent difficulties this would entail for JC Editions.

'I warned them that he wasn't like me', explains Stevens. 'Once he started I knew they'd have to put their feet down because not only would he do a terrific amount, he'd want them all printed right away. They wouldn't listen—and of course that's exactly what happened.

'In the next nine months he did something like 40 plates, which is an incredibly high output. I think some of his things would work better as lithographs because of the way he works with a pencil, but his way of working on a picture is ideally suited to etching.'

But while etching now filled most of Oxtoby's waking hours, he was aware that few (if any) galleries—especially the Redfern, with whom he now had a long association—would be interested in a show made up almost entirely of prints.

In 1974, while etching was commanding Oxtoby's almost undivided attention, Alex Postan offered him an outlet. Young, ambitious and desperately keen to represent Oxtoby, he offered him his gallery for a show of prints, spent a lot of time drumming up attention for the show and had a hit on his hands. David did a deal with Jim and John at JC Editions to halve the profits from the prints, and the success of the Postan-Oxtoby-JC Editions venture gave him the precious time he needed to embark on a series of rock paintings he now had mapped out.

By the beginning of 1976 the money had run out and David was in real financial trouble. Alex Postan had departed Britain, abandoning Oxtoby; JC Editions were finding it impossible to keep on producing the stream of etchings Oxtoby was giving them and he faced eviction from his flat for non-payment of rent. During one especially lean spell he was forced to stop injecting insulin—he just couldn't afford the food to balance it. He was forced to survive on £3 a week—and £1 of that went on food for Puddin', a beautiful stray cat he'd taken in the winter before.

Rescue came in the form of Joe Studholme, managing director of Editions Alecto. 'It was pretty amazing, actually', Oxtoby recounts. 'Joe offered me an advance, and agreed to pay my rent on the understanding that he would print any etchings I might do in the future.'

'It was an incredible gesture from someone I didn't know that well. So I joined Alecto and started on the series of Dylan prints and the two Elvis Presley etchings. I'll always stick by Joe—if someone helps you out like that, you stand by them forever. So I'm positively linked up with the Redfern and Alecto and I'm very happy with that arrangement.'

By mid-1976 Oxtoby knew precisely where he stood as far as his next show at the Redfern Gallery was concerned. They would have, by the beginning of April 1977, when they wanted to exhibit his new works, in the region of fifty pictures—paintings, prints, drawings and gouaches. And centre-piece of that show (entitled *Oxtoby's Rockers*) would be a giant Elvis Presley composition *The King—Fairground Sounds*. The first of what has now become a series of paintings with a central fairground motif, it was a bold and brilliant capturing of two essential Presley images—the rough hillbilly singer of 1957 and the smooth, glossy Las Vegas star of 1975. Other paintings which continue the theme and link rock'n' roll idols with the hurdy-gurdy-churning fluorescence of dodgems, waltzers, big dippers and candy floss stalls, are larger-than-life pictures of Little Richard and Fats Domino.

Very simply, the theory behind the fairground pictures is that of environment. With the exception of Radio Luxembourg, whose transmitter at the time was not big enough to give a clear signal to the whole of Britain, the main broadcasting of early raw rock 'n' roll was done from the loudspeakers of fairground rides. They pumped the music out while garish lights flashed and flickered and young men swaggered about trying to impress their dates and their rivals. David Oxtoby had been one of these young men, had soaked up the richness and excitement of the music and the sights. Now he was trying to recreate those days and pay tribute to them.

At the same time that the Redfern Gallery planned their show, Joe Studholme at Editions Alecto suggested that he might stage an exhibition of prints. The mammoth and excellent 13-plate Bob Dylan series had been printed and proofed, the two Presleys (echoes of the *Fairground Sounds* images) were finished, and Oxtoby had just completed work on *Rock Block*—a large 16-image print of Fifties rock heroes.

On 14 April 1977 the two shows opened, simultaneously and incredibly successfully.

The day before, David and I were at the Redfern Gallery for the installation of sound equipment which would relay taped Fifties rock 'n' roll into the Cork Street show for its run until 4 May. David was astride a wobbling ladder when the door opened and in walked Elton John, a long-time Redfern patron, purchaser of an Oxtoby painting of Rod Stewart from the Postan show in 1974, and invited to the opening next day.

I'd known Elton for a number of years and so introduced painter and subject (there were two Elton John paintings in the show). Elton

Oxtoby with, from top left clockwise, Roger
Daltrey, Rod Stewart, Jim Capaldi, Elton John,
Roy Orbison, and Kiki Dee.

wandered about for five or ten minutes and
then vanished downstairs to see John Synge
and Harry Miller, directors of the gallery. Five
minutes later he re-appeared, said how much he
liked the show and left.

A few moments after Elton had gone, John
Synge—looking extremely excited—approached
David. 'He's bought nine pictures', he said.
At the end of the two-week run, only fifteen
pictures remained unsold. *Oxtoby's Rockers* was
an outstanding success, commercially and critically.

One of the most satisfying aspects of the
show's reviews was the amount of real interest
and enthusiasm it received from the people
Oxtoby has been trying most to reach through
the years—the young rock writers who know his
subject matter by heart. While it has always
been satisfying to receive good reviews from
art critics on the technical merits of his work,
he has nevertheless been painting for other rock
fans as much as he has for himself. They can
see and understand much better some of the
allusions he makes in the pictures, and can also
understand references which are of necessity
lost on those who know nothing about rock
music.

In August 1977, an exhibition comprised of
some pictures left unsold from the Redfern
show, copies of all the Editions Alecto prints,
plus a number of paintings and drawings David
had kept back from both, went on tour in
Britain. Keeping the Redfern title it opened
first at the new Arts Centre in Chester (where a
record 5000 people flocked to see it during its
two-week run), moved on to the Wolver-
hampton Arts Centre (where the story was the
same) and closed—fittingly enough—at the
beautiful Cartwright Hall in Bradford.

As to the future, Oxtoby remains fairly non-
committal. He has already started work on
sketches for a number of new paintings—some
of them to be part of the Fairground Sounds
series.

And if some people are still slightly puzzled at
Oxtoby's single-mindedness when it comes to
subject matter, he has an answer which explains
why he will be painting, drawing and sketching
rock musicians for a long time to come:

'There are a lot of things I learned at the
Royal Academy, but the main one is that you
must enjoy your work. If you don't enjoy it, it
shows.

'And that's what most of my pictures are
about—enjoyment. I get the feeling there's too
much depression about these days, what with
one thing and another. So if I can give a little
pleasure to people, I'll have done what I want
to do.

'People get so bogged down with theories and
terminology, but I don't look at myself as a
painter in that way. I don't have any theories
or explanations of what I do. I just do it because
I enjoy it.'

The Critics

I first saw and became interested in David Oxtoby's work at the time of his first one-man show at Gallery One in 1963, when he was involved in the pop thing in a much less selfconscious way than anyone else. I think his unselfconscious willingness to plunge into his enthusiasms has been one of his strengths as an artist.

Music has always meant so much to him, but while one expects artists inspired by music to produce abstracts, he has never done so. He's been inspired by what could be called the jazz ideal, the idea of a painting as a riff, a quite spontaneous cadenza if you like, and he has the jazzman's attitude whereby final technical perfection isn't always as interesting to him as exploring different forms. If you look at the way his imagery moves, it's constantly bursting, budding and growing again.

His etchings have a refinement I hadn't seen in his work before, and I think his Dylan portrait is most elegant—I can't think of anyone in England who draws as well as that.

In America, I think there will be the same delighted response from people who are interested in popular music, whether professionally or because it's what they enjoy, as there has been in Britain.

Edward Lucie-Smith

Oxtoby's work has always conveyed an X-ray impact. Without sacrificing surface appearances he has been able to carry out visual surgery. An aspect, an element, or both, freed from natural environment suddenly take on extra emphasis.

Sheldon Williams
Art and Artists

I think drawing is his strongest medium because his drawings are usually the least selfconscious, when he's getting on top of an image, a subject or an idea. I think his etchings display the same quality—it's a very resilient technique and the images mature in a different way.

While his subject matter is obviously important to him, I find the strongest works are those where the importance of subject is held by the weight of the work itself. I don't think David or his subject matter are trivial—but at times he becomes over-literary, for which I do criticize him. But the fact that some critics find it hard, if not impossible, to get past his subject matter is their problem not his.

William Packer
The Financial Times, London

The music is rough and raw, so are some of the images and the ways of using paint and colour. Anything goes in the music, so anything goes on the canvas—so long as it serves the visual equivalent of the man and his music, of the rocker and his sound. If there is a haunted, sad look about many of the faces, it is more than a soulful pose; Oxtoby goes deeper than that.

Alan McPherson
Artscribe

David Oxtoby . . . has so wide a range of skills and resources in painting and technique . . . that he must, surely, become one of the most important painters in the immediate future of British art . . . He has the potential to fill a high place in painting over the next 20 years.

Richard Seddon
Yorkshire Post

The ICA had some distinctly vital variations on an abstract theme suggested by a group (*Traffic*) by David Oxtoby. They are wonderfully inventive and technically accomplished and the best—which to me means the most free—convey dazzling vibrations such as I imagine a drugged or drowning man might experience, an ecstatic fission of order.

Nigel Gosling
The Observer, London

David Oxtoby's work at first appears bizarrely strident. He is involved with a world compounded in terms of decibels, sweat and glitter . . . his work transcends a merely documentary function through the sheer brilliance of his technique and because he manages to romanticize each subject with a passion that is both tender and cynical.

Fenella Crichton
Arts International Magazine

. . . In the manner of the drawing there lies a remarkable sensibility that has captured the feel of the music—eye and ear become one.

Jonathan Morrish
Let It Rock Magazine, London

. . . You're left in no doubt that painter David Oxtoby is doing the right thing . . . in a way which truly reflects the spirit of rock 'n' roll . . . [he] paints very much in the living colours of rock. There are electric blues, terse acid greens, sharp and shocking pinks and violent aggressive reds. They shout at you in the same way as custom cars, neon signs, juke boxes and the stage lighting at a cheap package show. Even when the colours are muted they have the feel of Hammer horror or a faded Photoplay back number.

Mick Farren
New Musical Express, London

The key to Oxtoby as a painter is his overwhelming affection for his subjects; there is no distance, no sense of detachment that one feels in the approach of pop art painters, for instance.

Michael Watts
Melody Maker, London

GENE VINCENT: Craddock

Aquatec on cotton duck, 72 × 76 in.

Born Vincent Eugene Craddock in Norfolk, Virginia, on 11 February 1935, he left home at sixteen to join the Merchant Navy but was invalided out with a severe and debilitating leg injury four years later. He joined a Norfolk country band, was discovered by local disc-jockey 'Sheriff' Tex Davis who took demonstration tapes to Capitol Records, and was signed by them in their quest to find an answer to Elvis Presley. In 1957 Gene and his group, now called *The Bluecaps*, recorded and released the classic *Be-Bop-A-Lula*. It was a million-seller, was followed up by *Lotta Lovin'*—another gold disc. Changing fashions in pop and the emergence of sleek boy-next-door stars like Ricky Nelson, Frankie Avalon and Fabian made his brand of greasy violent rock *passé*, and Vincent all but

moved to Europe where he found new and bigger fame. Even so, his career declined even more and when he died of a bleeding ulcer in America (in 1971) he was beset by mounting financial problems.

Oxtoby: The initial idea for *Craddock* was to present Gene Vincent, the jukebox and microphone in a Fifties transport cafe with graffiti telling Vincent's life story. He had such a disastrous existence, I found the project too depressing to concentrate on the overall image, and had to rework the painting, dismissing my original concept.

LITTLE RICHARD: Speciality Fairground Sounds

Aquatec on canvas, 56 × 65 in.

Richard Penniman was brought up in Macon, Georgia, as a Seventh Day Adventist, and has a voice like a black gospel choir in full cry. His work in the mid-1950s has been dismissed as facile drivel, replete as it is with nonsense lyrics, but that is to miss the point of the man's incredible energy, verve, wit and ability to excite. In the early 1950s he recorded as a Blues singer for RCA, moved to the Texas-label Peacock, but in 1955 was signed to the famous Speciality company, was handed to producer 'Bumps' Blackwell as a project and together they cut seven million-selling records. Among the best-known Little Richard rock 'n' roll classics are *Tutti Frutti, Long Tall Sally, Slippin' and Slidin', Rip It Up, The Girl Can't Help It, Lucille* and *Good Golly Miss Molly*. In 1959 Little Richard retired from rock for the first time and returned to his religion, but in 1964

he re-emerged with the unequivocal rock 'n' roll of *Bama Lama Bama Loo* and was a hit again. His work during the late 1960s and 1970s has been spasmodic although he is still very much in demand by organizers of large festival events, where his outrageous camp style is still calculated to get people up and dancing—which is what rock 'n' roll is all about, after all.

LITTLE RICHARD: Little Big One ▶

Mixed medium, 29 × 19½ in.

Sunset Charly (top left clockwise): Junior Parker, Billy Lee Riley, Howlin' Wolf, Carl Mann, Warren Smith, Rosco Gordon

Indian ink base, each 17 × 17 in.

Oxtoby: Occasionally I am asked to create record cover. I consider this type of work on if I find the subject stimulating and then onl if I can retain the original art work. In this way I overcome subconscious barriers which may arise through commercial venture. I've found I am quite capable of doing a commissioned work—but usually the outcome is technically competent but gutles I set the above conditions so that I am in effect working for myself. The *Sunset Charly* series is a perfect example: Charly Records liked my Fifties series and I liked their Fifties series, so we agreed to get together on the Legendary Sun Performers records.

BIG BOPPER: Jape

Aquatec on canvas, 16 × 16 in.

Born J. P. Richardson in Sabine Pass, Texas, The Big Bopper was killed in the same plane carrying rock superstars Buddy Holly and Ritchie Valens from a concert in Iowa. He had enjoyed two hits (*Chantilly Lace* and *The Big Bopper's Wedding*) and recorded a number of unsuccessful country records. Best known as a fast-talking dee-jay on Station KTRM in Beaumont, Texas, he was also a songwriter of some repute, having penned Johnny Preston's No. 1 *Running Bear*. The real irony is that The Big Bopper should not have been on the plane at all—he had a stomach bug which made travelling in the tour bus a discomfort and Holly's protégé Waylon Jennings (then a member of the touring *Crickets*) gave up his place as a favour while guitarist Tommy Allsup gave his to Ritchie Valens.

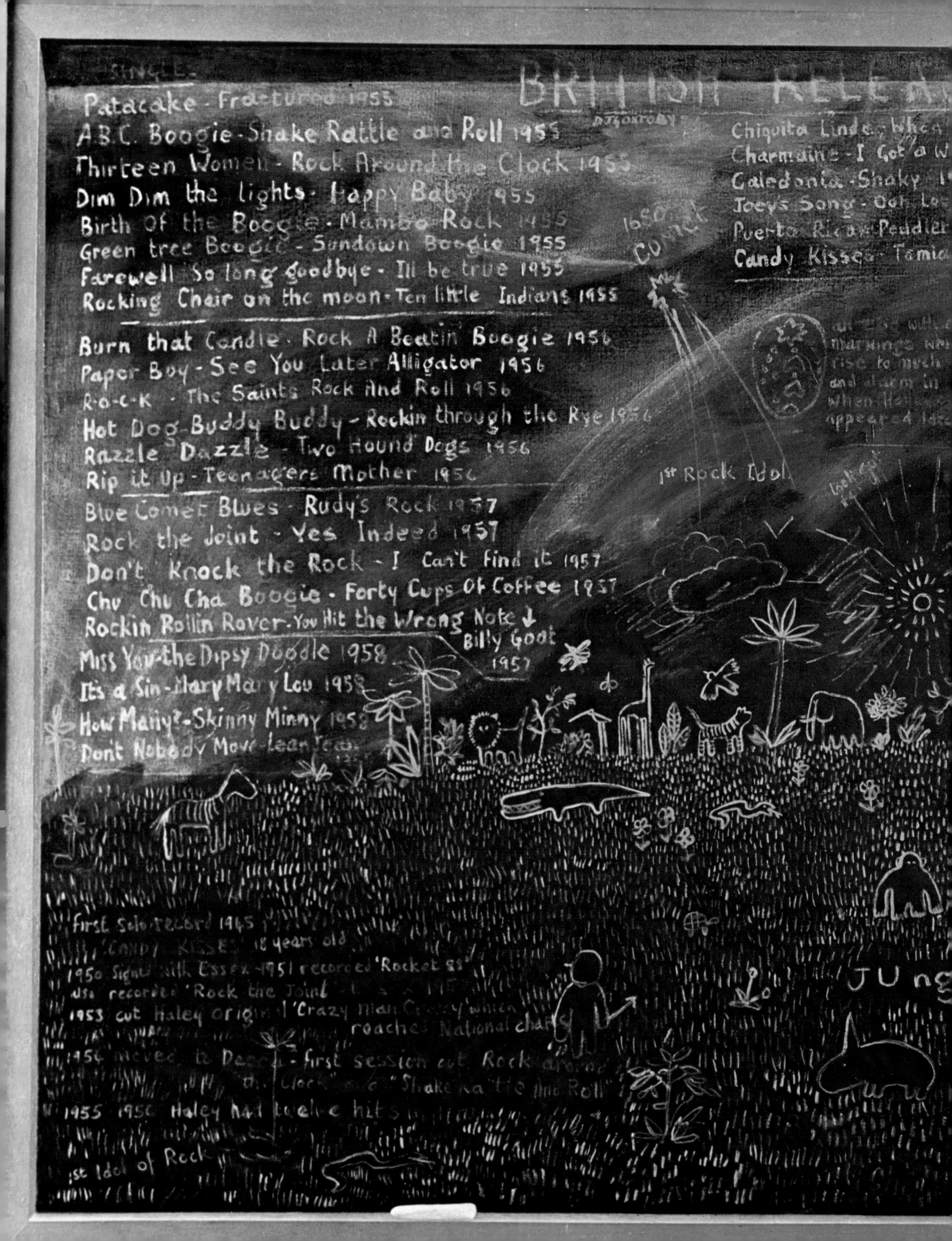

SINGLES

Patacake - Fractured 1955
A.B.C. Boogie - Shake Rattle and Roll 1955
Thirteen Women - Rock Around the Clock 1955
Dim Dim the lights - Happy Baby 1955
Birth of the Boogie - Mambo Rock 1955
Green tree Boogie - Sundown Boogie 1955
Farewell So long goodbye - Ill be true 1955
Rocking Chair on the moon - Ten little Indians 1955

Burn that Candle - Rock A Beatin Boogie 1956
Paper Boy - See You Later Alligator 1956
R-O-C-K - The Saints Rock And Roll 1956
Hot Dog Buddy Buddy - Rockin through the Rye 1956
Razzle Dazzle - Two Hound Dogs 1956
Rip it Up - Teenagers Mother 1956

Blue Comet Blues - Rudy's Rock 1957
Rock the Joint - Yes Indeed 1957
Don't Knock the Rock - I Can't Find it 1957
Chu Chu Cha Boogie - Forty Cups Of Coffee 1957
Rockin Rollin Rover - You Hit the Wrong Note ♪
                           Billy Goat 1957
Miss You - the Dipsy Doodle 1958
Its a Sin - Mary Mary Lou 1958
How Many? - Skinny Minny 1958
Dont Nobody Move - Lean Jean

BRITISH RELEA

DJ JOXTOBY

16 SOFT
COMET

Chiquita Linda - When
Charmaine - I Got a W
Caledonia - Shaky
Joey's Song - Ooh Loo
Puerto Rican Peddler
Candy Kisses - Tamia

1st Rock Idol

markings w
rise to much
and storm in
When Ha
appeared Ide

First Solo record 1945
CANDY KISSES 18 years old
1950 Signs with Essex 1951 recorded 'Rocket 88'
also recorded 'Rock the Joint
1953 cut Haley origin 'Crazy Man Crazy' which
                              reached National charts
1954 moved to Decca - first session cut Rock around
                     the Clock   'Shake Rattle And Roll
1955 1956 Haley had twelve hits

1st Idol of Rock

JUNG

1st Rock Idol

LLOYD PRICE

DUANE EDDY

BUDDY HOLLY: Fifties Buddy ▶

Mixed medium, 29 × 19½ in.

There's one real advantage to growing up, as Charles Hardin Holly did, in the city of Lubbock, Texas. Some of the best music can be heard there, whether it be country, Mexican or black in origin. A young man with enough of an ear to absorb these influences and draw on them discriminately can make some pretty fine music. Whatever else he did in the few years he was alive and playing, Buddy Holly did make fine music—most of which qualifies for the term 'timeless'. Originally signed to Decca, Buddy Holly recorded some fine rockabilly singles for them with no success. When they dropped him, he moved back to his home state of Texas and started recording at the New Mexico studios of local bandleader Norman Petty. With the impeccable support of guitarists Niki Sullivan and Sonny Curtis, bassist Joe Mauldin and drummer Jerry Allison (*The Crickets*) he cut a number of songs which Petty then sold to Coral Records. The first of those to be released was *That'll Be The Day*, which raced up the US charts to make No. 3, and to the top in Britain. This was followed by *Oh Boy/Not Fade Away*. Holly then went solo, had big hits with *Peggy Sue, Listen To Me, Rave On* and *Early In The Morning*, amongst others. He was bigger in Britain than America and despite repeated hits was seemingly groping for direction when he was killed in 1959, along with The Big Bopper and Ritchie Valens, when his small charter plane crashed soon after taking off from Mason City, Iowa, during a nationwide tour. A series of posthumous hits kept Holly in the charts until the mid-1960s, and he remains one of the most re-released artists of the rock era.

ELVIS PRESLEY

◄ **BILL HALEY: Film Credit Sound with Notes**
Aquatec on canvas, 36 × 47 in.

The first idol of rock 'n' roll, William John Clifton Haley was the most unlikely hero even in the mid-50s when his *Rock Around The Clock* rocketed to notoriety and gold disc status in 1955. He was chubby, thin of hair and already thirty years old. But the music was what sold Bill Haley to the millions of kids who flocked to see *The Blackboard Jungle* and a string of hits followed to boost *Bill Haley and The Comets* into superstardom. Born in Detroit, Haley grew up in Pennsylvania hearing and playing hillbilly country music, made his first solo record in that vein in 1945, worked as a disc-jockey and then formed his first group—*The Four Aces of Western Swing*. In 1951 he changed his style to the more aggressive rockabilly music of the south, had two singles (including the formative *Rock The Joint*) released, changed the group's name from *Bill Haley's Saddlemen* to *The Comets*,

recorded *Crazy Man Crazy* and reached the national charts. A move to Decca and the recording, as a favour to his manager who'd written it, of *Rock Around The Clock*, and the scene was set. The record was not a big hit, but was re-released after the follow-up *Shake, Rattle and Roll* reached the top ten in Britain and America. The rest is history. Among Haley's best-known records during his peak 1955–7 period are: *Burn That Candle, See You Later Alligator, R-O-C-K* and *Hot Dog Buddy Buddy*. He also made a string of rock exploitation films, including *Rock Around The Clock* and *Don't Knock the Rock*. Still very popular in Britain, which he visits regularly, he had a freak repeat number one single with *Rock Around The Clock* in 1974.

Oxtoby: *Film Credit Sound With Notes*—a classical rocker, Haley grows from a chalk mark. This painting is obviously based on *The Blackboard Jungle*, the film that can be given credit for spreading The Word. It took eight years of anatomical studies to create a rhino like the one depicted!

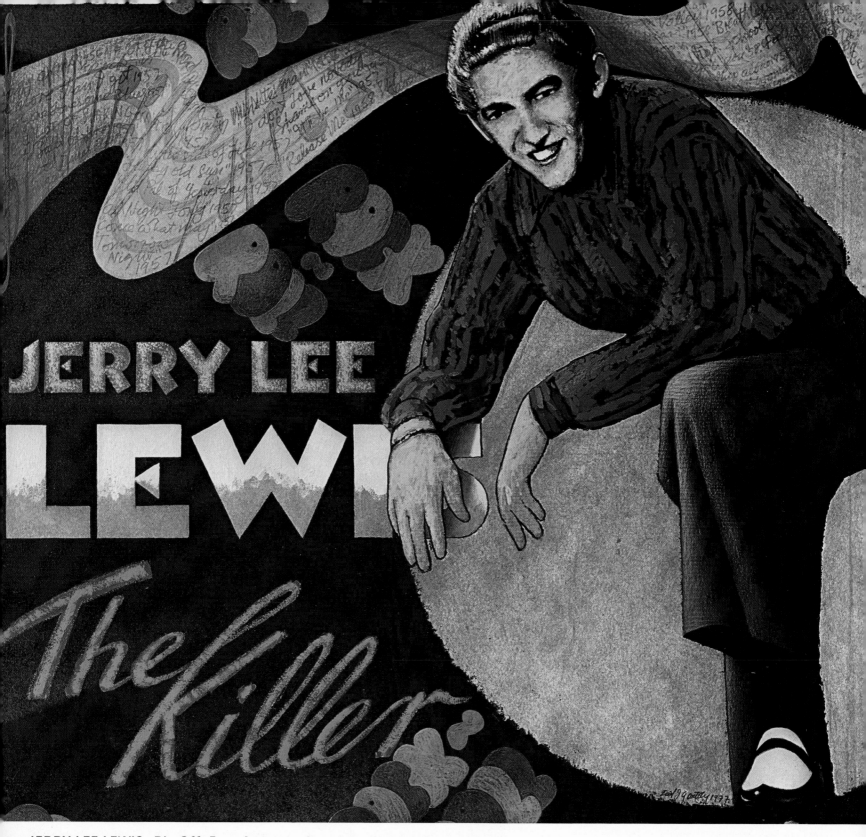

JERRY LEE LEWIS: Rip Off, Post Apart

Indian ink and gouache on brown paper,
19 × 22 in.

One of the original wild men of rock 'n' roll with his flamboyant boogie-style piano playing and outrageous on-stage antics, Jerry Lee Lewis was born in Ferriday, Louisiana, on 29 September 1935 and was taught piano by his father Elmo. He studied to be a minister at the Assembly of God Institute, Wazahatchie, Texas, while in his teens, grew homesick and returned home to play in a school orchestra and then in night clubs. Inspired by the success of Elvis Presley, he auditioned for Sun Records, was signed by Sam Phillips and had a good local hit with his first single *Crazy Arms*. In 1957 he topped the US and British charts with the classic *Whole Lotta Shakin' Goin' On*, and followed that with the equally successful *Great Balls of Fire*. After singing the title song of the hit film *High School Confidential*,

he became a genuine world star and enjoyed a string of hits. Public outrage over his marriage to a 13-year-old girl in 1958 set his career back and Jerry Lee started becoming something of a problem. He left Sun in 1963 and has made spasmodic attempts at a major come-back. The sad truth is that he remains the hero of a small following who still maintain he is what his nickname implies— The Killer. A great showman.

FATS DOMINO: (walking with) Mr D

Aquatec on canvas, 48 × 60 in.

Born Antoine Domino in New Orleans, on 26 February 1928, Fats Domino has been a recording star since 1948 when the Hollywood-based Imperial label signed him up. In 1949 he had his first million-seller with *The Fat Man* and since then has sold so many records he ranks third only to Elvis Presley and *The Beatles* on global sales. For the first six years of his career, Fats worked closely with trumpeter/bandleader Dave Bartholomew, writing a string of early rock classics which have stood the test of time and change. Most notable are *Goin' Home, Mardi Gras In New Orleans, Going To The River, I'm Walkin', Ain't That A Shame, Blueberry Hill, Blue Monday* and *Walkin' To New Orleans*. He remains the only musician successfully to translate the hybrid music of New Orleans into the mass market and is still active as a stage performer, sells incredible quantities of his huge catalogue, but has not enjoyed a sizeable hit since 1968, when he released a version of *The Beatles*'s *Lady Madonna*.

Fifties Sketchbook 3
Mixed medium, 37 × 26¾ in.

EVERLY BROTHERS: Rock in Fifties 9
Mixed medium (Indian ink base),
21½ × 18 in.

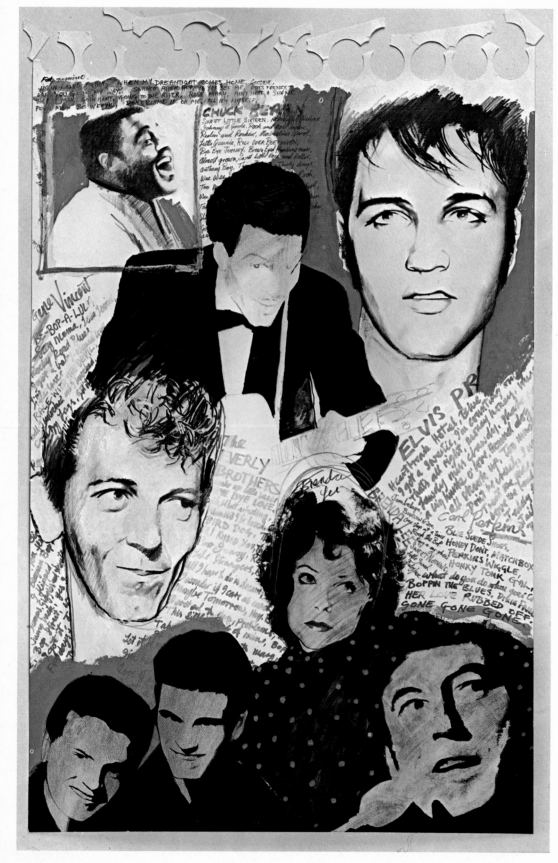

Bearing in mind that rock 'n' roll sprang as much from white country music as it did from black roots, the Everly Brothers (Don and Phil) personify the influence of the former. They took hillbilly music, up-dated it and found new songs (mostly written by Nashville husband and wife team Boudleaux and Felice Bryant) which would reach the new immense teenage market. That they were successful is beyond doubt—sixteen successive hits between 1957 and 1960 including *Bye Bye Love, Wake Up Little Susie, When Will I Be Loved, Bird Dog* and the archetypal misunderstood-teenager anthem *Problems*. Originally from Kentucky and born into a performing family (father Ike and mother Margaret had their own radio show), Don and Phil moved to Nashville in 1956 and were signed to Cadence Records in 1957 after a fruitless year at RCA. In 1960 they signed to the newly-formed Warner Brothers label in Los Angeles, had an immediate No. 1 hit with *Cathy's Clown* and followed that with *So Sad, Walk Right Back,* the weepy *Ebony Eyes* and *Crying In The Rain*. Stray hits like *Bowling Green* and *The Price of Love* kept them in the charts during the British invasion and domination of America, but their relationship deteriorated. In 1972 they went their separate ways and now pursue solo careers with Phil the more active and successful.

indian ink and gouache   *Rockabilly 2*   David Oxtoby 76

CARL PERKINS: Movie Magg 1954

Aquatec on canvas, 20 × 19½ in.

◀ **Fifties Sketchbook 4**

Mixed medium, 37 × 26¾ in.

The king of rockabilly—that distinctive fusion of black blues and white country music—Carl Perkins never achieved the stardom of contemporary Elvis Presley but nevertheless stamped his mark on the music of the mid-Fifties with a series of excellent hit songs (*Blue Suede Shoes*, *Boppin' The Blues* and *Dixie Fried* among them) and brilliant style-forming guitar work. Born in Lake City, Tennessee, he lost what chances he had of real stardom when he was injured in a car crash in 1956 and was therefore unable to appear on the famed Ed Sullivan TV show. In the Sixties he became an integral part of Johnny Cash's recording and touring team and more recently has enjoyed moderate success with a group which includes two of his sons. His early Sun recordings are still available and required listening for anyone interested in the roots of rock 'n' roll.

CHUCK BERRY: Mr B

Pencil drawing on layout paper, 27 × 36 in.

It's a measure of Chuck Berry's talents that two of the songs with which he is probably most associated—*Memphis Tennessee* and *Reelin' and Rockin'* —were not originally even on the 'A' sides of his many hits. Now acknowledged classics, they stand alongside other Berry masters such as *Maybellene, School Day, Rock and Roll Music, Sweet Little Sixteen, Johnny B. Goode* and *Little Queenie* (the list is almost endless), and are such an integral part of the vast tapestry which is rock 'n' roll music in the 1950s and 1960s that Charles Edward Berry is undisputedly a major figure. Discovered by bluesmaster Muddy Waters, who recommended him to Chess Records in Chicago, Chuck Berry's career spans two decades and innumerable musical styles, with his modern-day stage appearances still commanding huge audiences and great adulation. His main gift as a writer lies in his ability to encapsulate everyday situations into a line of song and to mirror the aspirations, dreams and problems of teenage America in a way which is the envy of countless other writers. He is also a consummate musician and a terrific stage performer.

CHUCK BERRY: Berry B. Goode ▶

Pencil and coloured pencil, $31\frac{1}{2}$ × $28\frac{1}{2}$ in.

Owner of one of the most distinctive voices in rock, Roy Orbison's peak period was between 1958 and 1965, when he recorded for the small independent Nashville-based Monument Records under the direction of label boss Fred Foster. During that time he recorded and had huge hits with a succession of big-sounding records, including *Only The Lonely*, *Runnin' Scared*, *In Dreams*, *It's Over*, *Dream Baby* and *Candy Man*, and built up a huge loyal fan following which still packs out the biggest auditoriums to hear him. A prolific song-writer (he wrote the Everly Brothers' hit *Claudette* for his wife who was killed in 1965 in a motorcycle accident). Tragedy struck again in 1968 when two of his three children were killed in a house fire. In 1977 he returned to Monument and recommenced working with Fred Foster. The British cover of the first album of the reunion (*Regeneration*) was painted by David Oxtoby.

CHUBBY CHECKER: Like We Did Last Summer

Mixed medium

Born Ernest Evans on 5 October 1941 in Philadelphia, he was discovered by his boss (a chicken market owner!) and recommended to Kal Mann, a staff writer with the local Parkway label. Signed to a long-term deal and re-named by TV-DJ Dick Clark's wife when she remarked that he looked like a young Fats Domino [get it?], he had a minor hit with his first single *The Class*, but really broke through when his version of *The Twist* became a smash hit. He followed it with a string of dance records over the next six years (*The Fly*, *Let's Twist Again* and *Pony Time* especially) and he had no fewer than 31 US chart entries from then until Parkway folded in 1968.

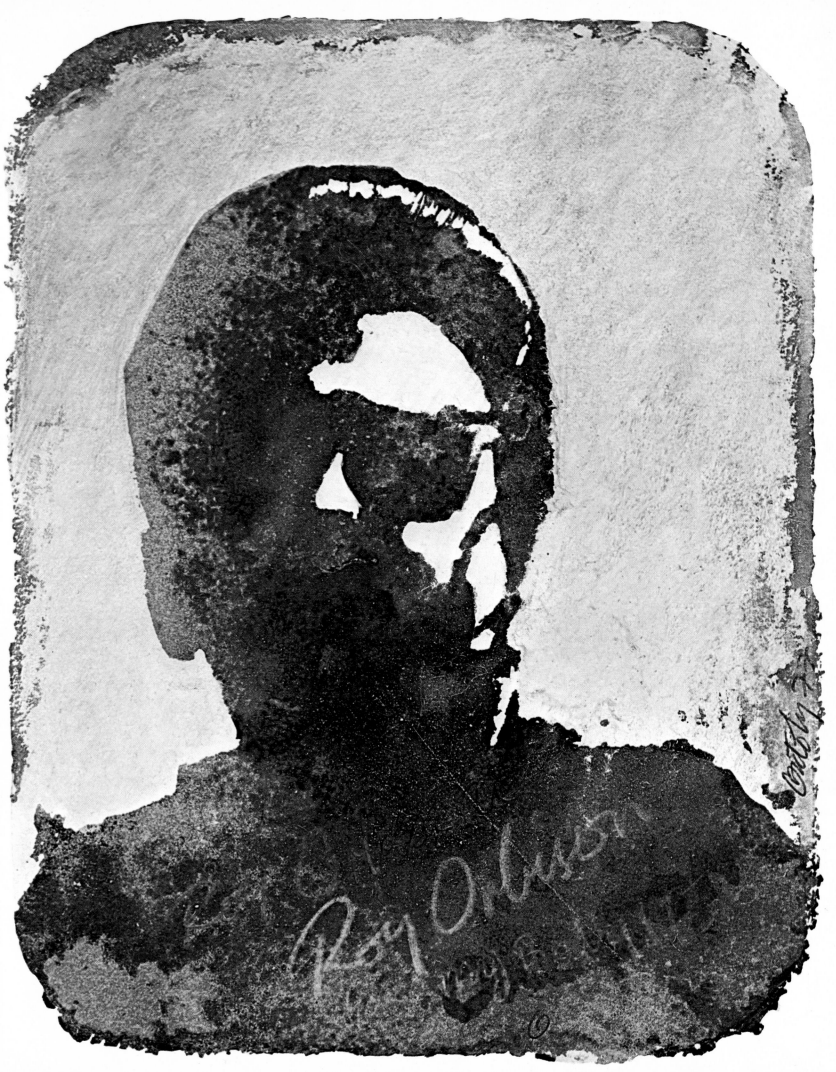

◄ **JOHNNY KIDD: Kid**

Mixed medium, 23 × 16 in.

Before the emergence of *The Beatles* in 1962, *Johnny Kidd and The Pirates* were the only truly authentic rock 'n' roll band Britain had ever produced. With their swash-buckling stage clothes, Johnny's eye-patch and a tough guitar-dominated sound, they enjoyed great popularity and hits in the shape of *Shakin' All Over* (now a rock classic and still performed by many other bands), *Hungry For Love, I'll Never Get Over You* and *Jealous Girl*. Born Frederick Heath, in Willesden, London, Johnny was killed in a car crash on 7 October 1966. In 1977 the members of *The Pirates* got back together playing new self-penned material and have garnered enough interest (and plaudits) to look like making it second time around.

EDDIE COCHRAN: Summertime 58

Aquatec on canvas, 48 × 60 in.

EDDIE COCHRAN: Summertime Reflections

Pencil, 36 × 27 in.

EDDIE COCHRAN: Summertime Gold ▶

Aquatec on canvas, 96 × 60 in.

Born Eddie Ray Cochran, in Oklahoma City in 1938, he grew up from the age of eleven in the Bell Gardens district of Los Angeles. It was there that he took up guitar and in 1954 became the accompanying guitarist to an obscure hillbilly singer Hank Cochran (no relation), eventually working with him as *The Cochran Brothers*. Country music was dropped in 1955 when Eddie saw Elvis Presley perform in a Dallas stage show and in 1956 he teamed up with song-writer Jerry Capehart, who then became his manager and secured him a deal with Liberty Records. They in turn found him a part in the movie *The Girl Can't Help It* in which he sang his famous *20 Flight Rock*. It was not this, but the smoochy *Sittin' In The Balcony*, which Liberty released as Eddie's first single, and it was a sizeable hit. Finding a follow-up proved a problem however, and it was not until September 1958 that *Summertime Blues* — a million-seller and now one of the classics of rock 'n' roll — was a hit. This was followed by songs like *C'mon Everybody, Weekend, Somethin' Else* and *Cherished Memories*, and appearances in two more films — *Untamed Youth* and *Go Johnny Go*. A much bigger star in Britain than in America, he was in 1960 in the middle of his first tour with long-time friend Gene Vincent when the car in which they were travelling from Bristol to London skidded and crashed. Cochran was killed, Vincent was badly injured . . . and the record high in the British charts just then was his *Three Steps To Heaven*. With Chuck Berry, Eddie Cochran remains one of the best commentators on American teenage life in the 1950s.

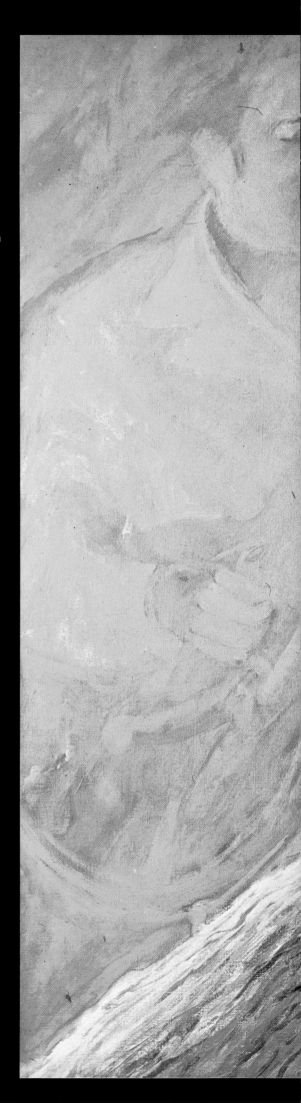

JIMI HENDRIX: Experienced Acquaintance; Electric Ladyland

Coloured etching, 12 × 8 in.; coloured pencil, 25½ × 19½ in.

What Elvis Presley did to the art of singing in the 1950s, Jimi Hendrix did to that of guitar playing in the 1960s. Quite simply, he did things nobody had ever attempted before with such style and skill that rock guitar was never the same again. Born James Marshall Hendrix, in Seattle, Washington, he grew up hearing the blues of people like Robert Johnson and Muddy Waters. In 1961 he joined the US paratroopers, was medically discharged in 1963 and started to make his living as a guitarist, playing with numerous backing bands for the likes of B. B. King and The Isley Brothers. In 1966, while playing under the name Jimmy James in New York, he was spotted by former *Animals* bass player Chas Chandler, who brought him to England and found a rhythm section in the form of Noel Redding (bass) and Mitch Mitchell (drums). *The Jimi Hendrix Experience*'s first single was *Hey Joe*, and was followed by the brilliant *Purple Haze*. In 1967, at Paul McCartney's insistence, Jimi was booked to appear at the Monterey Pop Festival and stole the show with his flamboyance and brilliance. Within months he was a superstar in his native land. In 1968 he had two gold albums with *Axis: Bold As Love* and *Electric Ladyland*, but by 1969 *The Experience* had broken up, Hendrix was arrested and charged with possession of narcotics in Toronto, and was subject to police harassment in New York. His last definitive stage performance took place in August that year when he appeared at the Woodstock Festival and played a now-legendary version of *The Star-Spangled Banner*. In the summer of 1970 he appeared at the Isle of Wight Festival and seemed strangely disorientated. He died on 18 September 1970 in London, officially of vomit inhalation following barbiturate intoxication. He deserved much better.

JANIS JOPLIN: The Good Years

Pencil and coloured pencil, 25½ × 19½ in.

'Texas is OK if you want to settle down', Janis Joplin once said of her home state, 'but it's not for outrageous people, and I was always outrageous'. That she was, preferring to live for the moment, cramming more into the four brief years she spent as a recording artist than most do in a lifetime. The freneticism was achieved at a terrible price, however, and in 1970 Janis died of a drug overdose in an Hollywood hotel room. Influenced early in life by Bessie Smith and Leadbelly records, she started singing country music and bluegrass but by the time she finally moved to San Francisco in 1966 to join the emerging *Big Brother and the Holding Company*, was the best white girl blues-singer ever. In 1968 she left *Big Brother* to go solo, was signed by Bob Dylan's manager Albert Grossman and had her first album *Cheap Thrills* sell more than a million copies in America alone. More albums followed, but it was for her raw dynamic stage act that Janis Joplin is most remembered. She could be brilliant or terrible, washed-out or child-like—but she was never mediocre.

Oxtoby: We used to meet down at the Bag O' Nails club. He was a shy, retiring fellow, very similar to Steve Winwood in that respect, seeming to conserve most of his energies for performances. It's this side of Jimi which dictated the mode of application for many of my works based on him—a kind of controlled freedom.

JIMI HENDRIX: Just Jimi ▶

Aquatec on board, 32 × 21 in.

DAVID BOWIE: Ziggy

Coloured etching, 8½ × 5½ in.

Arguably the most impressive rock figure to emerge in the 70s, David Bowie was born David Jones in South London in 1947, spent some time as a commercial artist in an ad agency and playing saxophone with local groups before joining Lindsay Kemp's Mime Troupe to learn the stage craft which was later to make his live appearances unforgettable. He recorded a number of unsuccessful singles for Pye and Decca (all redolent with an Anthony Newley influence) before the '67 flower-power phase jolted him into real action. The result was *Space Oddity*, the title track of which was to be a hit in 1969 and, when it was re-released in 1975, an even bigger one. He then ran the Beckenham Arts Lab in South London, was persuaded by Mercury Records to record again and cut the breakthrough LP *The Man Who Sold The World*. Demands for live appearances grew and he formed a band with guitarist Mick Ronson, bassist Trevor Bolder and drummer Woody Woodmansey (later to be known as *The Spiders From Mars*). The next two albums *Hunky Dory* and *The Rise and Fall of Ziggy Stardust and The Spiders From Mars* were acclaimed critically and launched Bowie into an extravaganza of action. *Aladdin Sane*, *Pin-Ups* and *Diamond Dogs* were the next three albums with Bowie immersing himself in the central characters they contained. Acting as producer he transformed the careers of Lou Reed (former singer with New York band *The Velvet Underground* in the 1960s) and ailing English rock band *Mott The Hoople*. In 1973 he quit stage work, moved to America, split from his manager, but re-emerged in 1974 with a new soul-based format. In 1976 he made *The Man Who Fell To Earth* film with Nicholas Roeg, won acclaim for his acting and has recently returned, in Britain and America, to concert stages.

DAVID BOWIE: Spiritual Pilgrim

Indian ink and pencil, 21½ × 30½ in.

Oxtoby: In the eighteenth century the spiritual pilgrim was a type of explorer from another world. During that period some people thought the stars contained forces similar to those in the human heart.

ELVIS PRESLEY: That's the Way it Was and Is

Pencil, 15 × 20 in.

The impact and importance of Elvis Aron Presley to popular music in the twentieth century is still being evaluated. That he turned the music business and the business of making music upside down when he emerged from poor-boy obscurity in 1954/55 is to understate ludicrously. Elvis Presley welded country music, rhythm and blues and gospel-shouting together and came out sounding unique. His appearance, with long hair, classic Greek god features and wild clothes, was also a revolution. Through initial local hits with Sam Phillips's Memphis-based Sun Records, he came to the attention of promoter/impressario Colonel Tom Parker and it was he, as manager, who was to sign Presley to RCA-Victor for a then unprecedented 35,000 dollars and guide his career until its end with Presley's death in his Memphis home in August 1977. The classic (even seminal) records Presley recorded still serve as an example of the pure excitement rock music should be. A string of mostly mediocre, but nonetheless hugely successful films occupied most of Presley's time in the 60s, but the 70s saw his return to stage work via a series of Las Vegas seasons and TV specials. However, they re-established his positions as a potent record-seller (something the emergence of *The Beatles* and their kin had dulled). His mysterious and reclusive life-style ensured that the Presley glamour never dulled, and his death was a thunderbolt to millions of people all over the world who had never even seen him live, but who had lived with the legend for more than twenty years.

ELVIS PRESLEY: American Trilogy, Fifties Sketchbook No. 2

Mixed medium, 37 × 26¼ in.

▲
ELVIS PRESLEY: Mr Rock 1956

Coloured etching, $11\frac{1}{4} \times 13\frac{1}{4}$ in.

◄ **ELVIS PRESLEY: Archive Fan Mag I**

Indian ink and watercolour on brown paper,
$22\frac{1}{2} \times 15\frac{1}{2}$ in.

ELVIS PRESLEY: Archive Fan Mag II

Indian ink and watercolour on brown paper,
$22\frac{1}{2} \times 15\frac{1}{2}$ in.

ELVIS PRESLEY: Sunspot ►

Aquatec on cotton duck, 60×48 in.

**ELVIS PRESLEY: Light and Movement
No 5 in E Sharp**

Aquatec and oil on canvas, 96 × 60 in.

◄ **ELVIS PRESLEY: The King—Fairground
Sounds**

Aquatec on canvas, 96 × 60 in.

Oxtoby: I have completed more pictures of Elvis than any other subject, the most recent being *The King—Fairground Sounds*. The initial concept for this painting came through my '*Light and Movement*' series. I began to get involved with movement through time along with various other aspects of light and movement. I also worked on the premise that in England in the 50s one could only hear good rock properly at fairgrounds. In order to express adequately my feelings for early rock, it's necessary to ensure that the mode of application and treatment in general reflect the freedom and often gutsy crudity of the subject, the instant appeal followed by a deeper appreciation as various intricacies surface with familiarity.

The King—Fairground Sounds deals with the question of realities, a juxtaposition of illusions, metamorphosis blending fact into fiction. Most of my pictures are concerned with this problem. After all, a lot of the early American rockers are mythical beings to the English. I use objective structures because

it's difficult to hear a voice in the abstract. My works use figures as one would use a coat-hanger. Accurate representation of the subject, technical variations, the theories and techniques I've developed over the years, are all secondary to an emotional response. Musical references, aspects of the subject's life (and occasionally my own) are sometimes suggested through imagery or a tactile surface value alone.

I realize my uncompromising attitude restricts response to my work but I believe you must live with your own truths or become a parasite on the ideology of others. Success is relative. Inner personal achievement should be uppermost and far more important than monetary rewards. I don't know where I'm going—you can only know that if you're following somebody else.

ELVIS PRESLEY: E. P. Rocker ►

Aquatec and oil on canvas, 60 × 48 in.

ELVIS PRESLEY : The Boy King   Coloured etching and aquatint, $26\frac{1}{4} \times 21\frac{1}{4}$ in.

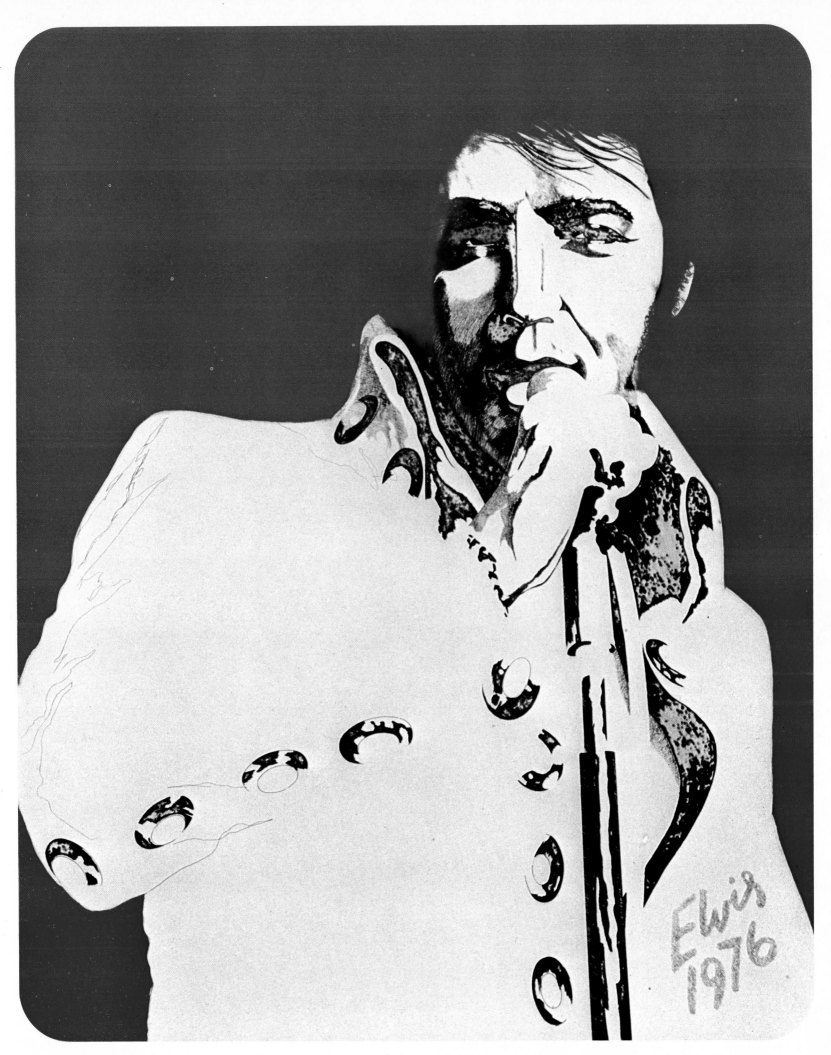

ELVIS PRESLEY: The King Coloured etching and aquatint, $26\frac{1}{4} \times 21\frac{1}{4}$ in.

HOWLIN' WOLF, STEVIE WONDER, RAY CHARLES: Blues and Roots

Pencil and coloured pencil, each
20 × 21½ in.

RAY CHARLES: Reflections on the High ▶ Priest

Aquatec on canvas, 96 × 72 in.

Howlin' Wolf

One of the Chicago-based bluesmen who so influenced white British R & B bands like *The Rolling Stones* (who recorded his *Little Red Rooster*), *Cream* and *Ten Years After* (*Spoonful*), *The Yardbirds* and *Manfred Mann* (*Smokestack Lightnin'*) and Rod Stewart (*I Ain't Superstitious*) in the early Sixties. Born Chester Burnett in Aberdeen, Mississippi, he was first recorded in the late Forties and early Fifties by Ike Turner and Sam Phillips (for Sun Records) before being signed by Chess Records in Chicago. He became a dominant force in the electrified city blues scene, and the debt owed him by British musicians was partly repaid in 1974 when, at the request of *The Rolling Stones*, he visited London to record a fine album with the likes of Eric Clapton, Steve Winwood, Ringo Starr and *The Stones'* own Charlie Watts and Bill Wyman.

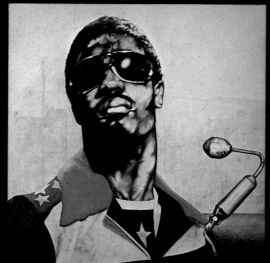

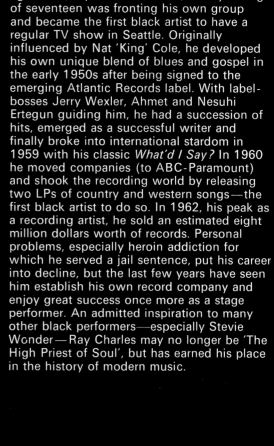

Born Ray Charles Robinson in Albany, Georgia, his early life was dogged by tragedies. He was blinded by measles at the age of six, orphaned at fifteen, but by the age of seventeen was fronting his own group and became the first black artist to have a regular TV show in Seattle. Originally influenced by Nat 'King' Cole, he developed his own unique blend of blues and gospel in the early 1950s after being signed to the emerging Atlantic Records label. With label-bosses Jerry Wexler, Ahmet and Nesuhi Ertegun guiding him, he had a succession of hits, emerged as a successful writer and finally broke into international stardom in 1959 with his classic *What'd I Say?* In 1960 he moved companies (to ABC-Paramount) and shook the recording world by releasing two LPs of country and western songs—the first black artist to do so. In 1962, his peak as a recording artist, he sold an estimated eight million dollars worth of records. Personal problems, especially heroin addiction for which he served a jail sentence, put his career into decline, but the last few years have seen him establish his own record company and enjoy great success once more as a stage performer. An admitted inspiration to many other black performers—especially Stevie Wonder—Ray Charles may no longer be 'The High Priest of Soul', but has earned his place in the history of modern music.

WILSON PICKETT: Pickett

Aquatec on board, 20 × 15 in.

Along with Otis Redding, the Pratville, Alabama-born Wilson Pickett probably best personifies the macho-soul period of the early-mid Sixties. With such hits as *In The Midnight Hour, Don't Fight It, Land of 1,000 Dances, Mustang Sally* and *634-5789*, he enjoyed a lengthy reign at the top of the soul tree. The end of that style of music and the introduction of more sophisticated and complex disco-styled music meant that Wilson Pickett—along with many who were most identified with the old sock-it-to-me material—went to the wall. In 1971 he had a big hit with *Don't Knock My Love*, and some success in 1974 with *Soft Soul Boogie Woogie*.

Bottom left:
JOE COCKER: Joe

Pencil and coloured pencil, 57 × 45 in.

Bottom right:
JOE COCKER: Cockerin'

Coloured etching, 7 × 2½ in.

One of rock's most identifiable voices, Joe Cocker was born in Sheffield, Yorkshire, on 20 May 1944. In 1964 he was signed by British Decca, released a flop single, toured Britain as support to Manfred Mann and returned to Sheffield to form *The Grease Band* with Alan Spenner (guitar), Henry McCullough (guitar), Kenny Slade (drums), Tommy Eyre (keyboards) and Chris Stainton (bass). Spotted by producer Denny Cordell, he was persuaded to return to London, and cut an unsuccessful single (*Marjorine*). His next single, a superb Ray Charles-styled cover of *The Beatles's With A Little Help From My Friends* made No. 1 in Britain and the US Top 40, and an album recorded in 1969 with such notables as Steve Winwood, Albert Lee and Jimmy Page, made him a star. Taken under the wing of American Leon Russell, Cocker was the star of a massive chaotic American tour entitled *Mad Dogs and Englishmen*, which ruined his health. In 1972 he was busted for possession of drugs while on tour in Australia, but got back together with Chris Stainton to record an album (*Something To Say*). His most recent recordings, the 1976 LP *Stingray* especially, prove that Joe Cocker is not finished even though he may be something of a casualty.

Oxtoby: Everything Joe does is believable, pouring emotional images into his work. Strong, powerful, often disturbing, he appears to live each word. *Joe* is the largest pencil drawing I've done to date. With it I wanted to present as many facets of his musical image as possible, like drifting visions while listening to a record. His demanding blues, gutsy, roaring, pounding and gesticulating, seem to be frustrated endeavours to penetrate even deeper into his own creativity. The main figure had to be taken from his performance of *With A Little Help From My Friends*—for me the first of an impressive list of superbly inventive interpretations.

▲ **STEVIE WONDER: Wonderfull**

Aquatec and oil on canvas, 20 × 24 in.

Oxtoby: Stevie has a natural talent. From his formative years he has had the ability to produce the unexpected in a relatively uncomplex form. When the development of a song seems traceable he introduces often subtle elements which lead in differing directions: intangible sequences on a figurative base presenting questions and puzzles.

Why the red line?

◀ **STEVIE WONDER: S'Wonderful**

Coloured etching, 6¼ × 5¼ in.

Born Stephen Judkins on 13 May 1950 in Saginaw, Michigan, Stevie Wonder survived the double handicap of blindness from birth and nine years as a child prodigy star to emerge as a dynamic and major talent in his own right. Discovered at the age of ten and taken to Tamla Records boss Berry Gordy by Ronnie White of *The Miracles*, Little Stevie (as he was then) had his first No. 1 record in 1962 with *Fingertips*. A string of hits and impressive LPs followed, including *Uptight*, *A Place In The Sun*, *I Was Made To Love Her* and *Yester-Me, Yester-You, Yester-Day*. In 1971 his career took a dramatic new turn with the release of his album *Where I'm Coming From*. This, and his next—*Music of My Mind* —which won acclaim from a huge rock audience, established Stevie as an important writer, arranger and multi-instrumentalist. Re-signed to Tamla in 1975 for an unprecedented twelve million dollars, he has in recent years been producing other artists, most notably B. B. King and Minnie Riperton.

◄ **OTIS REDDING: Oh 'tis Redding**
Pencil, 24 × 31½ in.

Less than six months before his death in a plane crash which also cost the lives of all but two of his band *The Bar Kays*, Otis Redding—already a huge soul superstar—played The Monterey Pop Festival and, with Jimi Hendrix, stopped the show. He was immediately acclaimed by a vast white American audience and was on the verge of achieving the world-wide recognition his talents deserved. Born in Dawson, Georgia, he grew up in nearby Macon and was inspired by local hero Little Richard. In 1962 he was working as road manager, driver and singer with *Johnny Jenkins and The Pinetoppers*, a local rhythm and blues band. Jenkins was recording some tracks at the Memphis Stax Studios and, when the session ended early, persuaded Redding to record one of his songs—*These Arms of Mine*. He was signed to the company's Volt label shortly afterwards and during the next five years had numerous big hits, best known of which are *Mr. Pitiful, I Can't Turn You Loose, I've Been Loving You Too Long* and *Fa Fa Fa Fa Fa (Sad Song)*. He was the most successful soul artist in Britain when soul music was the music of the mods and also fostered the careers of Arthur Conley and William Bell. When he died, he was enjoying his first American pop hit, the moody and atypical *Dock of the Bay*.

Oxtoby: Otis was the big one of soul. I was working on a painting of him when he died, as I was with Elvis when he died. In neither case did I complete the picture. This is the first painting I've done on Otis since 1967 and it's based on the raunchy side of him rather than the bluesy-ballad style. He's completely immersed in the raw excitement of his song—but then Otis seemed able to live every song and could pour emotion into everything he did.

OTIS REDDING: Oh 'tis the King
Pencil, 21½ × 31½ in.

OTIS REDDING: A Little Red in

Aquatec on board, 24 × 24 in.

ROBERTA FLACK: Flack

Aquatec on board, 15¾ × 21½ in.

Roberta Flack's early classical music training has resulted in her being one of the most stylish and articulate soul/jazz singers in the world. Born in Ashville, North Carolina, into a musical family, she attended Harvard University and completed degree courses in music and education before settling down in the early 1960s teaching in a segregated black school in North Carolina. Moving to Washington, she worked accompanying opera singers at the city's Tivoli Restaurant. In 1967 she quit teaching to concentrate full-time on music, was signed by Atlantic Records in 1969 and had a huge hit soon after with Ewan McColl's tender *The First Time Ever I Saw Your Face*. Her next big success was in 1973 with *Killing Me Softly*, though an album she recorded with Donny Hathaway in 1972 had given them a duet smash with *Where Is The Love?*. A perfectionist and stylist, Roberta Flack's recorded output is irregular but always impeccable.

Born Eunice Waymon, one of eight children, in North Carolina, Nina Simone was something of an infant prodigy and was playing piano by the age of five. She discovered formal music through the recordings of contralto Marian Anderson, learned to play jazz and was awarded a place at the Juillard School of Music. At the age of nineteen she made her first club appearance, was signed to RCA Records and in the late Fifties scored with a number of enthralling records, including *Don't Let Me Be Misunderstood* (later to be recorded, as was another of her hits, *I Put A Spell On You*, by British R & B group *The Animals*). She also recorded Billie Holiday's spine-chilling recounting of a southern lynching, *Strange Fruit*. By 1967 her involvement with the US black power movement was leading to even more overtly political themes and the alienation of the supper club audiences she'd once enraptured. She is now fully employed in black politics and makes only rare public appearances, and then usually at rallies.

NINA SIMONE: Nina and Mike ▶

Aquatec on board, 20 × 15 in.

ARETHA FRANKLIN: Aretha

Aquatec on board, 20 × 15 in.

The undisputed queen of soul music since the mid-1960s, Aretha Franklin was born in Detroit, one of five children of Reverend C. L. Franklin, himself a well-known figure in gospel music. Through her childhood and teens Aretha gained a reputation as a soloist with her father's travelling choir, but in 1960 branched out into the blues field, was signed to Columbia Records by John Hammond (the mentor of jazz queen Billie Holiday), but failed to click under his direction. In 1966 she moved to Atlantic Records and started to record with soul wizard Jerry Wexler, who did the trick. Her first record, *I Never Loved A Man The Way I Loved You*, sold a million, and this was followed by a string of gold discs. Among the numbers she is probably best known for are *Respect*, *Baby I Love You* and *I Say A Little Prayer*, while her emergence as a writer with *Think* was only the start of her domination of her field.

Born Pauline Matthews in Bradford, Yorkshire, Kiki Dee cut her musical teeth with dance bands in the north of England before moving to London in 1964 and teaming with songwriter Mitch Murray. For the next five years she recorded for the Philips-owned Fontana Records in the ersatz Tamla-Motown style so popularized by close friend Dusty Springfield. In 1970 she became the first white artist to be signed by Motown but failed to click with them, thanks to largely indifferent material. In 1972 she was approached by Elton John's manager John Reid (a former British head of Motown) who signed her to the new Elton-owned Rocket Records. Her first single for Rocket was a hit (*Amoureuse*) in Britain and Europe and her third single (*I've Got The Music In Me*) consolidated her new-found success by becoming a hit in America. In 1976 she and Elton John had their first No. 1 hit in Britain when they teamed up for *Don't Go Breaking My Heart*, and recent times have seen Kiki continuing to work with Elton as producer.

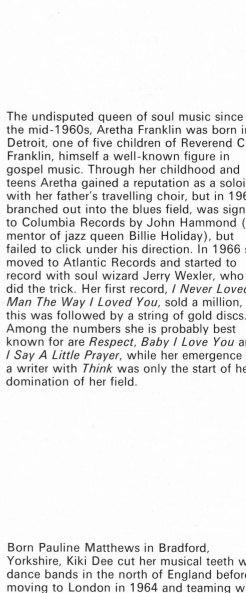

KIKI DEE: Kiki

Watercolour, 16½ × 13¾ in.

Coloured pencil and watercolour,
29½ × 21 in.

BOB DYLAN

Four etchings from a suite of 12 Dylan prints,
each 9¾ × 7¾ in.

Bob Dylan's influence, not only on his vast audience but also on other writers, singers and performers, is crucial to twentieth-century music. His lyrics opened up infinite possibilities to others who realized for the first time that politics could be poetry and that poetry could be rock, while his transition from folk singer to rock artist educated his audience to accept more varied music. Born Robert Zimmerman in Duluth, Minnesota, Dylan was influenced heavily by folk-politico Woody Guthrie in his early work. He moved to New York and gained a reputation in Greenwich Village clubs before being signed to Columbia Records by John Hammond. His second album *The Freewheelin' Bob Dylan* established him as the voice of the growing American folk/protest movement, and included such classics as *Masters of War, A Hard Rain's A Gonna Fall* and *Blowin In The Wind*. His next album *The Times They Are A-Changin'* consolidated his position and resulted in the unlikely (at that time) sight of a socio-political tirade being top of the pop charts. In 1965 he caused a furore by appearing at the Newport Folk Festival backed by the *Paul Butterfield Blues Band* and recording the electric *Highway 61 Revisited*. Working with *The Band* he further outraged folk purists, but in the face of his seminal '66 album *Blonde on Blonde* the consternation all but changed to admiration. A mysterious absence followed (said to have been forced by a serious motorcycle accident, although some doubt still exists about that story's veracity), but in 1968 he returned with *John Wesley Harding* and an obvious awareness of country music. In 1973 he starred with Kris Kristofferson in the film *Pat Garrett and Billy The Kid*, but it was not until 1975, with the superb album *Blood on the Tracks* that a completely unflawed Dylan album was released, and in 1976 he was again on top form with *Desire*.

BRUCE SPRINGSTEEN: U.S. Ahead

Coloured pencil and watercolour, 26 × 26 in.

BRUCE SPRINGSTEEN: He's the One

Aquatec on cotton duck, 96 × 48 in.

Born on 23 September 1949 in New Jersey, Bruce Springsteen learned his craft in New York's Greenwich Village, commuting regularly to play guitar at Cafe Wha, and then founding and leading a number of New Jersey-based bands. In 1972 he was taken by his then manager to meet John Hammond (the legendary A & R man whose thirty-year career included production signing of artists as diverse and important as Billie Holliday, Aretha Franklin, Peter Seeger, Bob Dylan and Leonard Cohen). Hammond signed him to CBS and Springsteen's debut album— *Greetings From Asbury Park, N.J.*—was released in January 1973. His second LP *The Wild, The Innocent and The E Street Shuffle* was hailed as a masterpiece and in 1976 when his *Born To Run* set was released, Springsteen became the first non-political figure ever to appear on the covers of *Time* and *Newsweek* in the same week. Only time will tell whether Springsteen is as important as his PR men claim.

Oxtoby: *He's the One* was inspired by *She's the One* from Springsteen's third album *Born to Run*. A cold, almost clinical piano introduces the song, which builds into a cacophony of Americanisms. Springsteen fights against the city he's part of, producing a curious combination of emotions. I used sky and buildings to reflect the piano sequence, while an overall zigzag structure and an uneasy yellow provided the conflict as well as something of the feeling of an American city.

Founder-member with Steve Winwood, Chris Wood and Dave Mason of English superband *Traffic*, James N. Capaldi was born in Worcestershire of Italian descent, played with a number of local bands before striking up a friendship and working partnership (he wrote lyrics for Winwood's songs) with the other members of *Traffic*. Between 1967 and 1974 he and Chris Wood were, with Winwood, the nucleus of a band which shrank and grew with alarming regularity, but which was always incredibly popular—especially in America. In 1972 he recorded a solo album *Oh How We Danced* in Muscle Shoals Studios, Alabama, with that studio's famous session team. Its reception encouraged him to return to the studios in 1974 to record his second solo effort *Whale Meat Again*. In 1975, a year after Winwood finally decided to call a halt to *Traffic*, Capaldi recorded the LP *Short Cut Draw Blood* and had a hit in Britain with a re-working of Roy Orbison's classic *Love Hurts*. A superb drummer and increasingly-accomplished singer, Jim Capaldi's main donation to British rock in the 1960s has nevertheless been as lyricist for Winwood, most especially on the best *Traffic* albums—*Mr. Fantasy*, *Traffic*, *Last Exit*, *Low Spark of High Heeled Boys* and *On The Road*.

Oxtoby: Jim's powerful attack and delivery belies his often beautifully sensitive lyrics. His albums are superbly produced feats of musical emotional dexterity, worthy of a founder-member of *Traffic*. However, as with many bands, to appreciate Jim's talents fully one should see him in concert. Visually, he is reminiscent of a fiery gypsy with a carved face. In the etching *Rock On JC* I have tried to portray this romantic Romany during a live performance. He's at ease with the blast-furnace of his environment, adrenalin-pumping, enjoying completely the heat and sounds of his own creation.

JIM CAPALDI: Rock on JC

Coloured etching, 11¾ × 8½ in.

JOHN LENNON: English Rock

Aquatec on canvas, 36 × 36 in. First state.

If John Lennon had stopped writing and playing when *The Beatles* disbanded in 1970 after seven years at the top, he would still lay claim to a place in the rock music hall of fame for the wealth of superlative songs he co-wrote with Paul McCartney. As it is, his work since then has been patchily brilliant and has only served to underline his genius. A volatile, witty and often cynical man and writer, John Lennon's active political life and sometime involvement in the *avant-garde* art world (he is married to Japanese artist Yoko Ono and has recorded a number of experimental albums with her) have often led him into deeper and hotter waters than he could have dreamed existed, but his undoubted sincerity and genius invariably save the day and his reputation. He now lives in America and is as capable of surprising,

astonishing and thrilling the world now as he ever was. The original working-class hero and aware of it.

Oxtoby: This painting is no longer as depicted (nothing to do with English rock). I decided to rework certain sections a little and the result is now in America, the property of Bernie Taupin.

Above left:
VAN MORRISON: Into the Mystic

Pencil and coloured pencil, 27 × 18 in.

Above right:
VAN MORRISON: Listen to the Lion

Pencil and coloured pencil, 27 × 18 in.

STEVE HOWE: Howe's That?

Pencil, 15½ × 22 in.

To have recorded one album which is considered by all but a churlish few to be one of the top ten essential rock records of all time is something of a feat. That Van Morrison has recorded two (*Astral Weeks* and *Moondance*) makes him somewhat unique. Born into a working-class family in Belfast, Ulster, he grew up with the vast jazz and blues collection of his father to listen to. By the age of thirteen he could play guitar, saxophone and harmonica, and by the time he was sixteen he'd left school to work as a musician with a rhythm and blues band, *The Monarchs.* In 1963 he formed the group *Them,* came to London and in 1964 had hits with *Baby Please Don't Go* and *Here Comes The Night,* while *Gloria* (a *Them* standard) became a non-hit classic. In 1967 he disbanded *Them* and moved to America to work with producer Bert Berns. One of their first recording sessions resulted in the American Top Ten hit *Brown-Eyed Girl.* When Berns died of a heart attack later that year, Morrison signed with Warner Bros. Records and in the summer of 1968 recorded *Astral Weeks* in a straight forty-eight hours. It is an album of great beauty, combining impressionistic lyrics with Morrison's Celtic romanticism. In 1970 *Moondance* was released and established Van Morrison for all

time as a rock figurehead, and the early 70s saw him record seven more superb albums, the most notable of which are probably *St. Dominic's Preview* and *Hard Nose The Highway.*

Oxtoby: I try to show Van's dreamlike quality in my works, the combination of Irish unpredictability, lyrical mysticism and the noncomformity of American blues. Van writes some beautifully descriptive pictures. When Picasso was asked: 'How do you draw?', he replied: 'You just close your eyes and sing.'

MICK JAGGER

Pencil and Indian ink. One of a series

▲

MICK JAGGER: Bloody Altamont

Aquatec and pencil on paper, $31\frac{1}{2} \times 43\frac{1}{2}$ in.

If any one man was the epitome of the articulate generation which emerged in Britain in the 1960s and proceeded not only to ask salient questions about politics and social mores, but publicly to kick over the traces, it must surely be Mick Jagger. *Enfant terrible* of the British rock scene and leader of *The Rolling Stones*—arguably the best rock 'n' roll band in the world for more than a decade—he came to represent everything that was frightening to older generations. Born Michael Philip Jagger, in Dartford, Kent, he spent some time at the London School of Economics before dropping out to form *The Stones* with Brian Jones, Keith Richard, Charlie Watts and Bill Wyman. Launched in a blaze of publicity and recurring scandal, they became—with Jagger as their main spokesman and figurehead—a dominant and driving force, behind which a whole generation massed. An accomplished writer (with partner Keith Richard) of some essential rock songs—*I Can't Get No Satisfaction, Let's Spend The Night Together,*

Get Off My Cloud, 19th Nervous Breakdown, Honky Tonk Women, Brown Sugar being but a few—he has brushed with authority on numerous occasions, made a number of films, avoided active politics like the plague and now suffers the slings and arrows of gossip columnists and new-wave bands.

DIANA ROSS: Supreme Lady ▶

Coloured pencil, $15\frac{1}{2} \times 22$ in.

Oxtoby: For this picture I accepted a photograph almost at face value and worked on the piece as a technical exercise. Occasionally I feel the need to stretch the eyes alone and work on a composition obviously close to the edge, just to see how far I can push it without going over.

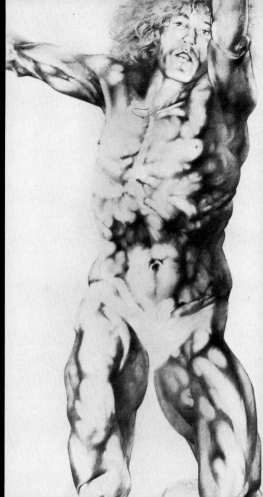

ROGER DALTREY : Who's Who

Pencil and coloured pencil, 40 × 28 in.

Top right:
ROGER DALTREY : Tommy Buonarotti

Pencil, 37 × 26¼ in.

Above right:
IAN HUNTER : Overnight Angels

Pencil, 18 × 18 in.

Opposite page:
ROGER DALTREY : Little Who

Pencil and coloured pencil, 10 × 9 in.

As lead singer with *The Who*, the only British rock band from the 1960s to be still functioning without a change in personnel or popularity, Roger Daltrey has been acknowledged as one of the best and most exciting vocalists in rock for the past ten years. With his renaissance looks and hard, immediately-identifiable voice, he's acted as the ideal model for any number of youngsters and music critics. In 1973, as *The Who* began to slacken off on concert work and settle down to a more relaxed working pattern, Daltrey recorded a solo LP, *Daltrey*, and had a huge hit with the Leo Sayer—David Courtney song *Giving It All Away*. Cast in the title role in Ken Russell's film of *The Who*'s classic rock-opera *Tommy*, Daltrey impressed Russell enough for the director to give him the lead in *Lisztomania* in 1976. Daltrey's solo recording activities were continuing meanwhile with *Ride a Rock Horse* and the founding of his own record company.

Oxtoby: *The Who's* contribution to English rock is unquestionable. It's undeniable that Pete Townshend is the major inspirational force but Daltrey provides the figurehead. I became aware of the extent of Roger's range only after hearing his first solo album, *Daltrey*, which was produced by Adam Faith. This particular record has influenced my vision of *The Who* ever since. Maybe this argument is merely an excuse for me to continue using Roger's hair as a device to convey movement and musical flow . . . but I still love you, Tommy!

ELTON JOHN: Candle in the Wind

Pencil and silver pencil, 30 × 25 in.

ELTON JOHN: Bernie's Mate ▶

Aquatec on canvas, 30 × 25 in.

Whatever his claims to fame as an accomplished pianist and writer (with lyricist partner Bernie Taupin), Elton John is owed a mighty debt by the world's concert-goers as the man who brought fun back to a rock music scene threatening to commit hara-kari by that most deadly of weapons—self-righteous seriousness. With his wild clothes and outrageous spectacles, Elton made having a good time popular again—and in the process became one of the richest performers in the world. He also, along the way, did collaborate with Taupin to write some timeless pop and rock songs, and produce some of the most polished and successful albums in the history of pop. Born Reginald Kenneth Dwight, in Pinner, Middlesex (he later changed his name by deed poll to Elton Hercules John), he worked originally as a tea-boy for a music publisher, but eventually joined R & B band *Bluesology*, which backed numerous visiting US stars and became the full-time band for British blues star Long John Baldry. In 1967 Baldry decided to move over to cabaret work and Elton started working with Bernie Taupin (as a result of a 'new talent' ad in pop paper *New Musical Express*). They languished, writing to order, for two years before following their own noses. Elton's second LP *Elton John* started the real breakthrough which was achieved fully with *Tumbleweed Connection*. This also contained the hit *Your Song* and was followed by American superstardom via albums like *Madman Across The Water, Honky Chateau, Don't Shoot Me, I'm Only The Piano Player, Goodbye, Yellow Brick Road, Caribou, Captain Fantastic and The Brown Dirt Cowboy, Rock of The Westies* and *Blue Moves*. The latter was his first for his own Rocket Records label. An avid soccer fan, he is chairman of British team Watford and a board member of the LA Aztecs. In 1975 he made his screen debut as The Pinball Wizard in *Tommy*.

Oxtoby: England's Mr Showbiz! As with the best art forms, Elton's work can be appreciated on many levels. There's a curious fusion of numerous influences in his music, from the lavish Forties' Hollywood musical and the Fifties' pumping rock piano, to the depth and clarity attained by expert use of modern production techniques. In *Bernie's Mate* I wanted to reflect this combination of musical forms. The solidity of the head melts away, becoming part of the backing. This background, through a mixture of irridescent greens, represents the shimmering epoch of Hollywood while the freer rock element is projected into the spectacle frames, the inner parts of which give depth and an added dimension. I wanted him to sit on the canvas like the Rock of Gibraltar.

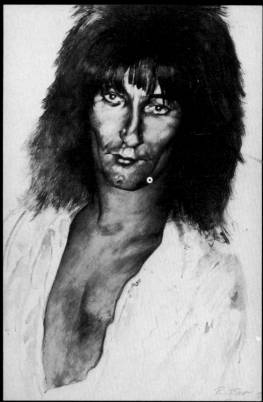

ROD STEWART: Every Picture Tells a Story

Watercolour, $40\frac{1}{2}$ × $28\frac{1}{2}$ in.

Born in London on 10 January 1945, Rod Stewart started his post-school life as an apprentice footballer with Brentford FC, but hated the menial tasks he was required to do and left to go on a hitch-hiking tour of Europe with English folk artist Whizz Jones. In 1965 he joined the British R & B band *Hoochie Coochie Men* to sing joint lead vocals with Long John Baldry, with whom he then formed *The Steam Packet* (with Brian Auger and Julie Driscoll). *Shotgun Express* was his next band and this was followed by the *Jeff Beck Group*. Beck's success in America meant newfound fame for Stewart, who in 1969 joined the survivors of *The Small Faces* to found *The Faces*. A successful songwriter, Stewart emerged as a solo superstar from his five years with *The Faces*, and in December 1975 he announced his intention of going solo. He now owns his own record company, Riva Records, and has become prime gossip-column material, thanks to his outlandish jet-set lifestyle. At his best, Rod Stewart remains one of Britain's best-ever rock singers.

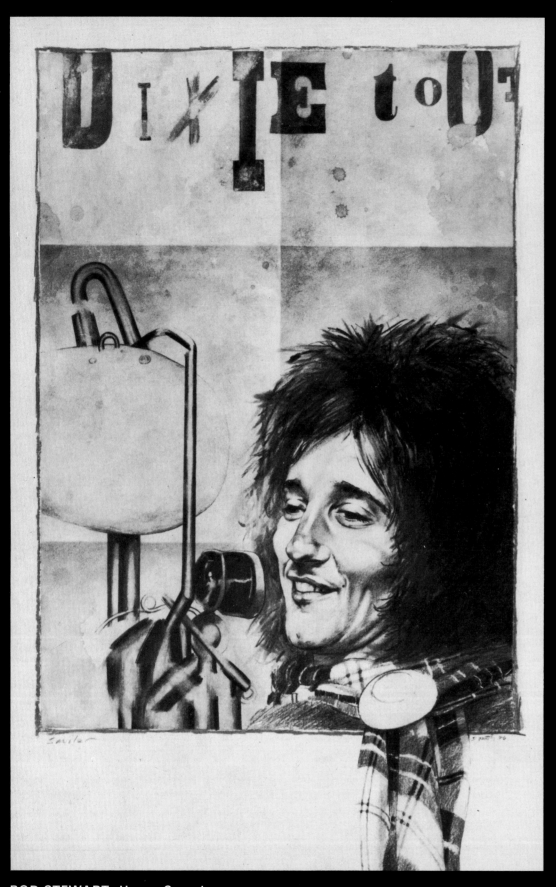

ROD STEWART: Happy Sounds

Pencil and coloured pencil, watercolour and coffee, 30 × 20 in.

ROD STEWART: Royal Scot

Coloured pencil, 13½ × 15 in.

Oxtoby: *Royal Scot* tries to convey the weight and coarse aggressive flow from the Stewart/Beck era, while showing the clarity and sharp edge of a seasoned performer. *Every Picture Tells a Story*, although also dealing with Rod's interpretation of the Blues, shows another aspect of the star. Rod thought these works were too sombre, and so I did a picture called *Happy Sounds* to placate him. Based on *Dixie Toot* from *Smiler*, this is a real *Boy's Own* drawing. Our beaming hero wins through despite the antique microphone.

PAUL McCARTNEY: Yesterdays With a Blue Guitar

Aquatec and pencil, 43½ × 31½ in.

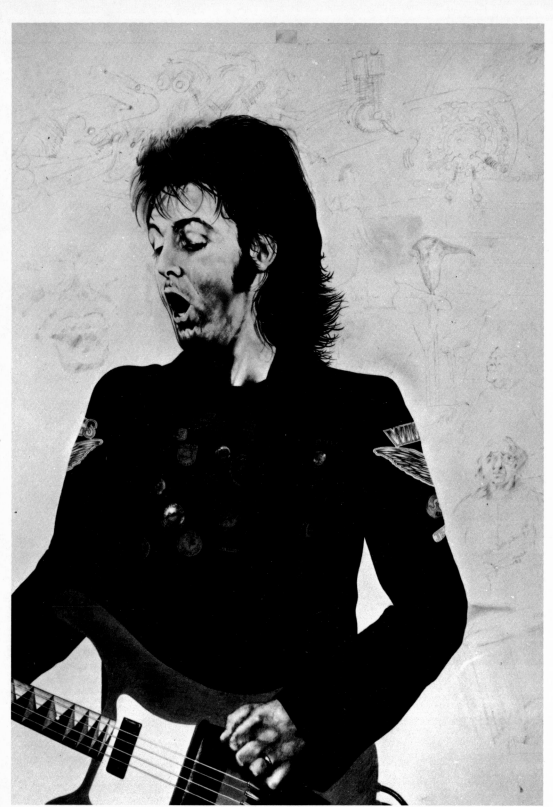

Of the four Beatles, Paul McCartney has emerged as the one with the best knowledge and control over his own musical and commercial destiny. Acrimony over *The Beatles'* breakup cast him in the role of hard-bitten villain and his first few albums, while selling very well, were vilified as pap by critics. Marriage to Linda Eastman gave him other priorities and time to think, plan and develop, and in 1972 he returned to full active public service with the hugely-successful and artistically-impressive *Red Rose Speedway* album. From then on it was all upwards movement as McCartney, along with Linda and their band *Wings*, took flight. In 1973 they released *Band On The Run*, in 1975 the excellent *Venus and Mars*, while 1976–77 saw *Wings At the Speed of Sound* dominate sales and popularity charts all over the world. Paul McCartney is still one of the best craftsmen in popular music, is reputed to be one of the highest-paid recording artists ever and is known to control the biggest independent group of music publishing companies ever assembled under one man's roof.

Oxtoby: *Yesterdays With A Blue Guitar* is a combination drawing of Paul with my yesterdays. The background contains drawings based on the works of many of my friends while badges scattered across Paul's chest have names of other friends. The drawing was born out of a conversation with David Hockney who told me he was working on a series of etchings based on a poem inspired by a Picasso painting. I figured one thing missing from that sequence was a drawing!